This Garden of Death

(The History of York Cemetery 1837-2007)

Hugh Murray

A lovely flower
removed, alas how soon
from the tender watchful care
that had reared and cherished it
to be the FIRST transplanted
into this garden of death
yet not to continue here for ever
but at the appointed season to be taken
into the paradise of God
There to revive and flourish
In perfect and unfading beauty

Epitaph on Grave of Charlotte Hall,
Buried in York Cemetery 21 January 1837

Set in Minion Pro 12pt

Prepared by:

York Publishing Services Ltd
64 Hallfield Road
Layerthorpe
York YO31 7ZQ
Tel: 01904 431213

Website: www.yps-publishing.co.uk

To the volunteers, the 'unsung heroes', who have unstintingly given their time and skills to ensure that the cemetery continues to be an asset for the use and enjoyment of the citizens of York

Acknowledgements

The production of this history would not have keen possible without the help of many people. Dr Richard Keesing, the chairman of the Cemetery Trust, and his fellow trustees. have given me their whole-hearted encouragement originally to write and, later, to extend and enhance this history. The original objective, in 1991, was to improve our knowledge of the activities of the York Public Cemetery Company but since then much has been achieved under the ownership of the Trust. As a result a new chapter has been added covering the years since 1991 and new material has been inserted in the original six chapters. These earlier chapters were given full references to the many scattered sources from which the history was compiled in lieu of the records of the meetings of the managing committee of the Cemetery Company which were deliberately destroyed prior to its demise. The new chapter, however, has none. This is because it is entirely drawn from the minute books of York Cemetery Trust and the Friends of York Cemetery, and my own personal knowledge as a trustee and treasurer of both organisations for almost the entire period.

In York City Archives, where many of the cemetery records are now housed, Rita Freedman, and her colleagues have, as always, attended to my demands with unfailing helpfulness. The same courtesy has been extended to me in York Reference Library by the staff there when consulting the files of York newspapers. Dr Bill Fawcett has given my amateur attempts to produce plans, showing the development of the cemetery, a more professional appearance. The indefatigable David Poole in his tireless searches in newspapers and other records has produced many titbits of information which have enhanced the cemetery story. Peter Hanstock, Helen Kirk, Richard Keesing. Ray Hawkshaw of the York Corps of the Salvation Army and Mrs Alma Winship, the daughter of George Jackson, the last cemetery foreman, have added considerably to this history by producing many of the photographs which I have used as illustrations. Lastly I must record my gratitude to Van Wilson who has painstakingly read through the manuscript to eliminate my idiosyncrasies and errors of grammar, punctuation and orthography.

By the same author

Introduction

It is with great pleasure that I introduce you to Hugh Murray's excellent and now considerably extended history of York Cemetery. The trustees requested Hugh to review his first history of the cemetery to celebrate the 20th anniversary of our owning the entire site and we were delighted he felt able to carry out the further research required although in this instance the material was somewhat more easily come by than during his first historical study. Few except that dedicated band who write historical accounts will appreciate the enormous labour such work entails. The vast amount of detail contained within these pages has been gained from many hundreds of hours pouring over old news papers, council records, company minutes and listening to the accounts of many local people. The task of obtaining this information was made so much more difficult by the fact that the original cemetery company destroyed large quantities of its own records before going into liquidation in 1966. That which is now known has come to light through painstaking examination of newspaper reports going back to the early part of the 19th century.

The first six chapters of this history which cover the period from 1830 to 1990 were researched and written in little more than a year and it is clear that this excellent work would not have been written without Hugh's dedication and altruism. Although I have been associated with the cemetery for many years a great deal of its history was completely unknown to me and I have been both encouraged and dismayed in equal measure from what I have learned from Hugh's work. If one is unaware of the mistakes of the past it is impossible to avoid these mistakes. Whether one learns from them is another matter, however ignorance of them can only make their compounding more tragic. From Hugh's researches it is clear that there were farsighted individuals associated with the company who realized the dire consequences of certain actions which would not become evident for almost a century. Greed and a short sighted desire for profit, however held sway and in combination with other factors, led remorselessly to the fateful day in June 1966 when the gates to the cemetery were closed for the final time by York Cemetery Company. Even at this point there was hope for a better future for the site, but the dead hand of officialdom ensured, in the end, that nothing positive would come from the liquidation. And thirteen miserable years later the whole site, or what was left after its having been stripped of everything which could be sold, devolved to The Crown. The 24 acres of sacred burial land, having now lost its freehold, returned to the state of 'bare legal title', a state which it had had almost one thousand years earlier when William the Conqueror seized all the land in this country by act of conquest. The final devolution to the Crown must be considered as the most miserable day in the whole history of this once fine site. At this moment all rights of access and use were lost to those citizens of York and elsewhere who had purchased them in good faith and in the belief that they would hold them in perpetuity. But in fact all was not lost and life and hope have returned. New people with new visions are once more present to guard the new freehold title.

A further fifteen years have passed since Hugh wrote the first part of this history and one must admit to a certain level of satisfaction in seeing the considerable progress which has been made in establishing a more healthy long-term financial future for the cemetery. All the buildings have been restored, the boundary walls renovated and in places rebuilt and the great gates restored and reinstated. Our very able and dedicated architect Ron Sims very sadly died a few months after completing the restoration of the catacombs beneath the chapel last summer. Over the years several good and loyal trustees have taken their places with the immortals and our chief benefactor and great supporter Donald Shepherd has also gone forth upon his final journey. However we still enjoy the generous support of his wife Pat who has been a great source of encouragement to us all over many years. Further we have been fortunate in having a well-balanced and excellent group of trustees with considerable skills in law, financial management, accountancy and ecological land management amongst other important attributes who have given their time and expertise in a spirit of altruistic service to the community. Over the years The Friends of York Cemetery have been a great strength and support for the work of restoration, education and land management, contributing large sums of money to the whole project. Amongst many other activities they run an extremely successful programme of guided walks and tours of the cemetery. And underpinning the whole venture is the exceptionally skilled and dedicated group of volunteers who go largely unsung. Without their generosity of spirit and sense of commitment to the greater good, little of any value would have or could have been achieved.

Richard Keesing, Chairman, York Cemetery Trust

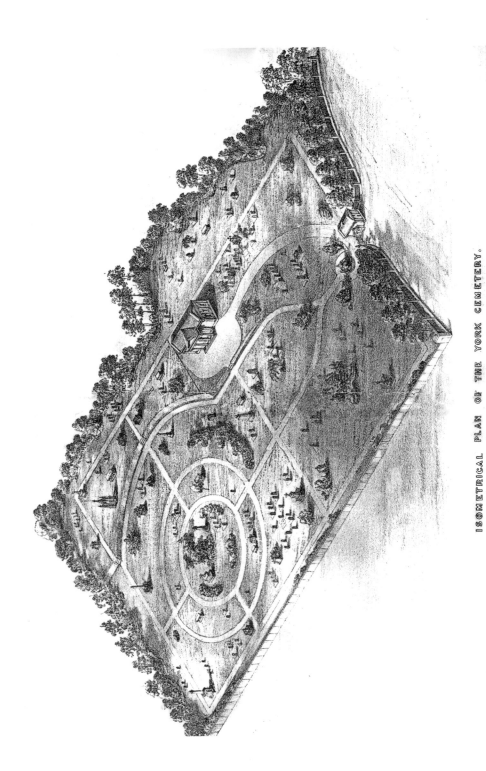

An isometrical plan of York Cemetery in 1843 drawn by the architects, Pritchett & Son

1: 'Gardeners, Ditchers and Gravemakers' – The Formative Years

*'There is no ancient gentlemen but gardeners, ditchers and gravemakers;
they hold up Adam's profession.'*

Hamlet V i 32

'The *main object* of a burial-ground is, the disposal of the dead in such a
manner as that their decomposition, and return to the earth from which they
sprung, shall not prove injurious to the living; either by affecting their health,
or shocking their feelings, opinions, or prejudices.' These are the words of John
Claudius Loudon, landscape gardener and writer on gardening, agriculture and
architecture, written in 1843, shortly before his death.[1] In 1837 York had achieved
this desirable objective when the York Public Cemetery Company opened its
cemetery but before then burial conditions in the city were the very antithesis of
London's definition.

At the beginning of the 19th century decadence was rapidly overtaking York.
It no longer had the status of a northern metropolis which it had enjoyed in
the previous century. The changes in habits and manners which had taken
place throughout the Kingdom were probably felt more severely in York than
in most other places and, as a consequence, the amount of capital expenditure
diminished.[2] The Corporation's neglect of the Ouse navigation added to the
already high price of coal, brought to the city in boats from the West Riding, and

prevented the establishment of factories. Commercial progress was hindered by the requirement that anyone trading in the city had to be a freeman. There were no industries of any size and the largest group of workers was in domestic service. Nevertheless, despite this decline in its fortunes, the population was expanding; from 16846 in 1801 to 28842 in 1841, an increase of 71%. Large as this may seem, in the same period the increase in the manufacturing towns in the industrial West Riding was much greater – Leeds 186%, Huddersfield 247% and Bradford 444%. York's sole role was parasitic, as a market, a place where produce from the countryside around could be brought for sale and where goods and services were sold.

During the 18th century the population, living almost entirely within the walled medieval city, had remained constant for the first 60 years and then, in the last four decades, rose by about 4000, a natural increase, largely unaffected by migration, which continued into the first four decades of the next century. The inevitable consequence was increasing poverty and overcrowding, particularly in the lower Iying areas of the City near the Ouse and Foss. The Corporation complained in 1810 'that the poor were not being properly supplied with work and were becoming highly burdensome with a steady increase of expenditure on poor relief'.[3] But, in any case, not all the poor could work. They lived in densely populated, badly ventilated courts, with communal privies and water supplied, either from a tap in the yard for a limited period each day except Sunday or drawn direct from the rivers. Bad sewerage and drainage, bad water, air made foul by rotting refuse and the presence of immense heaps of night soil whose liquid content leached into the rivers, all contributed to the unhealthiness of the working class. Sickness prevented them working and made them even poorer, unable to feed and clothe themselves properly. As a result the death rate among the poor was high. The expectation of life of a labourer and his family was 23.75 years while the gentry and professional people could enjoy, at 48.62 years, more than double this. Although the health of the city improved gradually in the first 40 years of the 19th century the death rate in 1840 was still 26.51 deaths per 1000 population, more than double the present (2007 – 10.9). During this period an average of 525 bodies had to be disposed of every year.[4]

For centuries the dead of York had been buried in the graveyards of the medieval parish churches, supplemented later by the burial grounds of the Quakers on Bishophill (1667), the English Presbyterians (Unitarians) in St Saviourgate (1793) and the Congregationalists in Lendal (1816). Because of pressures on the land within the city the parish graveyards were necessarily small and had been buried many times over. In some cases they had been made even smaller by the building of houses on them to raise additional revenue for the parish; for example, Lady Row (1316) at Holy Trinity, Goodramgate, and a row of cottages (1337), built in St Sampson's churchyard. It was impossible to dig a grave more than three or four feet deep and even then many bones and human remains from previous interments were disturbed, 'a gross indecency towards the dead'. To overcome this problem earth was brought from the outlying districts and heaped on the burial grounds to deepen them. The surfaces of many churchyards were thus considerably above the level of the streets and the floors of the churches. Evidence of this practice can still be seen at All Saints, North Street and Holy Trinity, Micklegate, amongst others. In spite of this, and before city centre burials had ceased, many unedifying and undignified sights were reported. Putrescent human remains were observed in public thoroughfares and it was not uncommon to see bones lying about. But what was worse was the stench of decomposition perceived in the streets and the tainting of the water supplies by the drainage from the graveyards.[5]

Many diseases, including typhus and cholera, were attributed to the noxious miasmas emanating from graveyards. Loudon was very specific: 'To inhale this gas, undiluted with atmospheric air, instant death; and even when much diluted, it is productive of disease which commonly ends in death... '[6] Even if modern researches have proved that the gases of decomposition are not harmful[7], their constant presence round the grave yards was nauseating and made the grave digger's work, in particular, extremely unpleasant, with the result that drunkenness was endemic amongst them. This state of affairs gave cause for concern to many of the prominent and public-spirited citizens of York but it took a major epidemic to start the process of improvement.

In 1826 a cholera pandemic spread from Bengal taking three years to reach Persia and Afghanistan before following the caravan routes to Russia and then continuing on to arrive in Germany in 1831. The first case in the British Isles was recorded in Sunderland in September 1831. The disease appeared in London in February 1832, missing out many of the towns and cities in between, but by November it had spread throughout Britain. York was alerted by an Order in Council issued by the Privy Council in October recommending that Boards of Health should be appointed from magistrates, clergy and doctors who were to find a house in which the sick could be isolated, prevent contact with those affected by the disease, and arrange for all old paper and rags to be burnt, the drains to be cleaned and the roofs of houses lime-washed. By November a York Board of Health had been set up. It immediately embarked on the task of preparing for the inevitable – the arrival of the epidemic in the city. The first victim, Thomas Hughes, a waterman who lived at Hagworm's Nest in Skeldergate, died on 3 June 1832. By 22 October cholera had disappeared from York leaving 185 dead out of the 450 people who had contracted the disease.[8]

One of the major problems for the Board of Health had been to find a suitable burial ground where the victims could be interred at such a depth that their infected bodies would not provide a further hazard to the citizens. A survey of graveyards was made and sent to the Privy Council to call to its attention the very crowded state of all of them and the great difficulties the Board was having in protecting the living from infection from the dead. In some churchyards it was difficult to find a place to bury a body and in others graves could not be sunk to a greater depth than three or four feet. Further alarm was raised by the fact that the most crowded burial grounds were in the most populous parts of the city closely surrounded by `thickly peopled dwellings of the poorer and middling classes'. Only in St Mary's, Castlegate and old St George's churchyards was there sufficient room to bury any parishioners who succumbed to the disease. Quite apart from the immediate need for a place where cholera victims could be buried safely, it was the hope of the Board that their report would ultimately lead to the formation of public cemeteries in the vicinity of the city for each of the four wards.

Although they had first considered a piece of land close to Walmgate Bar, objected to by the Quakers who had a school nearby, the Board did not find a solution to their problem until some victims had already been buried in their parish churchyards. This, with a burial service in the church, was the right of every parishioner and even after the Corporation had granted a piece of ground, near the City's dog kennels outside the Bar Walls between North Street Postern and Micklegate Bar, where the funeral rites and burial could be performed in the open air by the victim's own parish clergyman, considerable prejudice against interment there had to be overcome.[9] The relatives of victims had been assured that, in giving up their rights to a parish burial, the bodies, wrapped in cloth saturated in pitch, would never be disturbed but the Corporation decided in July that the land would only be granted for 20 years. In August, however, it was agreed to give a lease to the Archbishop of York for 60 years but, after getting a ruling from London that the consecration, eventually performed on 23 January 1833, could not be made for a limited period and had to be in perpetuity, the sanctity of the cholera burial ground was secured, although an unsuccessful attempt was made to secularise it in 1925 for road widening.[10]

The cholera epidemic had produced a flurry of activity in York. 'The men in power and the better classes in general became alarmed for their own safety, they gave some attention to the undrained and filthy condition of the localities and abodes of the lower classes, and made some temporary efforts to remove the evils'[11] but once the disease had run its course and disappeared the York Board of Health was dissolved and the epidemic quickly forgotten. Nevertheless some of its members were determined that the citizens of York should be provided with a place where they could he given a dignified burial with the prospect of their remains, once interred, never being disturbed.

Shortly after the cholera burial ground had been consecrated a number of individuals of different religious denominations met in the Savings Bank in St Helen's Square to discuss `the best means for remedying the inconvenience arising from the crowded state of the churchyards in York'. A committee was formed of four legal gentlemen, solicitors Jonathan Gray, James Richardson junior, and James Russell, and barrister Thomas Barstow, and the Revd John Acaster, Vicar of St Helen's, Stonegate, who had all served on the Board of Health. After numerous meetings and various inquiries they published a circular, in June 1834, inviting subscriptions towards the establishment of a cemetery for the City.[12] This, as the press was to comment, in wishing the enterprise success, was a project `well calculated to remove a great evil and to confer a considerable benefit on the City.' Most of the churchyards were crowded and scarcely capable of receiving any more bodies – a state of affairs which had particularly concerned the Board of Health during the cholera epidemic. The Revd John Acaster had a lease from the crown on three acres of land near the Malton Road and had already applied for this to be transferred to the committee. It was proposed that a lodge and offices, a chapel for divine service and a house for the officiating minister should be erected on the land which was to be enclosed. At the same time Acaster was trying to raise and endow a church, urgently needed for the large population of Layerthorpe and Heworth (not realised until 1869). Should this be successful the cemetery chapel would not be necessary and the savings made could be contributed to the church.

The cost of providing the cemetery and buildings had been calculated at £3000 which the committee hoped would be raised by 120 shares of £25 each. As an incentive, prospective shareholders were to be entitled to a brick vault made to contain four coffins. The Archdeacon of York, the Venerable Robert Markham, who had consented to the provision of such a cemetery, was to set the scale of charges for all but the poorer classes who were to pay the average of what they were currently paying for burial, and incidental expenses, in their own parish churchyard. While this new cemetery was to be open to all funerals it was hoped that separate cemeteries would eventually be provided for Walmgate and Micklegate Wards.[13] What the Archdeacon really wanted was four cemeteries not three, with separate ones for Monk and Bootham Wards. On hearing this the committee suspended their activities to leave the Archdeacon free to progress his plan. He had hoped to obtain land from the Government but, because of the scarcity of suitable land, he had to abandon his idea.

Jonathan Gray, having been elected an alderman on 31 December 1835, suggested that if the Corporation possessed any land suitable for a cemetery then the common objective of both the committee and the Archdeacon could be achieved to the great benefit of the public. Accordingly, on 8 February 1836, the Council directed its finance committee to inquire and report on what Corporation land could be 'conveniently applied to the purpose of a Public Cemetery or Cemeteries'. The finance committee's deliberations were somewhat protracted; they took until 6 May to decide that a parcel of land called Old Bayle situated near the City gaol and a close of land, formerly part of Heworth Moor, near the windmill occupied by William Hesp, would 'not be unsuitable'. Three days later, however, the Council, with very little vested interest within its ranks (only three councillors out of 36 and three aldermen out of 12 were to become shareholders or trustees of the Cemetery Company), decided to postpone any discussion on the finance committee's report and thus lost an opportunity to gain a foothold in the management of the arrangements to be made for the disposal of the City's dead.[14]

Immediately after the Council had taken this decision two York solicitors, Thomas Hodgson and W.S. Campion, published a prospectus proposing the flotation of the York General Cemetery Company. It opened with such a forthright statement that they found it necessary to stress that it was not an exaggeration: -

> In few places in the kingdom are the above evils [those which attend burial places] so conspicuous as in the City of York, with its Burial Places in the central and most populous parts of the City – confined in space – surrounded with buildings – and crowded with dead. The inhabitants of houses adjoining most of the Church Yards can bear testimony to the

revolting scenes that continually occur in them, where scarcely a grave is made to receive the body of one person without disturbing that of another, and exposing the remains of departed relatives and friends in a manner offensive to the senses – shocking to the feelings – and prejudicial to the health of the inhabitants.

So opposed was this to what J.C. Loudon had in mind that one wonders if he had read it before arriving at his definition of a burial ground.

It was proposed to form a joint stock company to provide, on an eligible site in the immediate vicinity of the City which was available at a moderate price, only one cemetery for 'the Interment of the Dead in the Suburbs in the City of York ...... sufficiently large for the wants of the City, for the reception of persons of all classes and of all religious denominations'. The capital was to be £10,000 in shares of £10 each, to be applied for by 11 June by which time 10s 0d per share was to be paid. Nobody, however, was to be allowed to hold more than 20 shares. By this provision it was hoped to dispel the suspicion that the motives of the company and prospective shareholders were financial and not altruistic; the revenue obtained by such an investment was stated to be a secondary consideration. Nevertheless the prospectus drew attention to the dividend of 17½% then being paid to the shareholders of Rusholme Road Cemetery, Manchester, only just opened.[15]

The establishment of public cemeteries to make money out of death was a 19th century phenomenon. The first large metropolitan public cemetery laid out on modern lines was Pere Lachais in Paris while in this country the Revd Thomas Drummond, a Presbyterian Minister, established Rosary Burial Ground in Norwich in 1819, using his small reserves of capital in a personal sacrifice to remedy the unsatisfactory situation in Norwich churchyards. He bought five acres of former market garden land and vested it in a trust to ensure that its use was guaranteed for all time. A further eight acres were added in 1903 and with its graves generously spaced out on a hillside site, planted out with trees and shrubs, it is a haven of tranquillity still meeting its founder's wishes.[16] The next public cemetery, established, as all others were to be, on less altruistic lines than Rosary, was Liverpool Necropolis formed in 1825 as a joint stock company, followed four years later by St James Cemetery, Liverpool, which only one year later was to pay its shareholders an 8% dividend.'[17] Thereafter cemetery companies were formed in towns and cities throughout the kingdom, some by special Act of Parliament and others merely by a Deed of Settlement. The prospectus of the York General Cemetery Company listed those at Manchester, Birmingham, Leeds, Newcastle upon Tyne and Sheffield in addition to Liverpool.

As soon as the York General Cemetery Company made its plan known the original committee suggested that the two bodies meet to discuss the best mode of progressing their common objective. This offer was declined and, as it appeared that the new contenders in the field had no specific plans for implementing the ideas in their prospectus, the original committee decided to hold a public meeting at which they could inform those persons likely to unite with them of the scheme which they had been maturing since 1833.[18] At this meeting, held at the Savings Bank on 1 July 1836 under the chairmanship of Alderman Jonathan Gray, it was resolved `to form a cemetery or burying place, which shall be situate without the walls, but adjacent to the City, and open to all persons of all religious denominations; who shall be allowed to inter their dead, according to their respective views of the rites of sepulture'. This cemetery, to be called York Public Cemetery, was to consist of 'a competent plot of ground, laid out in an appropriate and ornamental manner'.

The Capital of £6,000 was to be raised in 600 shares of £10 each, with an initial deposit on application of £1 a share. Again, to stress that the objective of the company was the public benefit and not personal profit, no individual was to hold more than five shares except by bequest or inheritance but, to encourage shareholders, they were told that experience of similar institutions had shown that they might expect 'a fair and even liberal remuneration'. The subscription list was to remain open until 1 August. The land, with part consecrated `according to the rites of the Established Church', and buildings, including a chapel where funeral services could be celebrated by the dead person's own minister, were to be conveyed to trustees to ensure they were used forever for their intended purpose. The trustees and committee of management were to be chosen with one half from members of the Church of England and the other half from members of other religious bodies. A plan of the burial ground, with the situation of every vault and grave, and a register of the death, age and description of every individual interred were to be kept and to be open for inspection in the same manner as parish registers. The committee was to set the prices of graves and vaults but no charges were to be made over the actual cost of interment for people dying in houses or tenements rated under £5 a year. A small provisional committee of eight members was appointed to publicise these resolutions and call a meeting of shareholders.

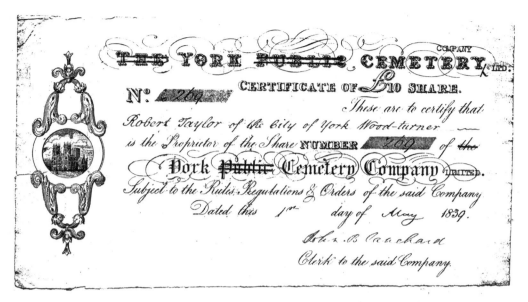

A share certificate issued by the York Public Cemetery Company to Robert Taylor, a wood turner, on 1 May 1839. It has changed hands on a number of occasions and has also been amended to show the changed status of the company in 1945.

[Courtesy of Mrs. Hyde]

The shareholders' meeting of what was now called York Public Cemetery Company was held at the Savings Bank on 18 August under the chairmanship of William Cockburn, Dean of York. He was later to become a fierce defender of the literal interpretation of *Genesis* for the Creation of the Earth against the scientific theories of the British Association for the Advancement of Science culminating in his publishing *The Bible defended against the British Association* in 1844. The provisional committee reported to the meeting that half the shares had been applied for by persons who, considering the project to be of public benefit, had no particular view to profit. Had not the number of shares for each person been restricted to five many more would have been taken and it was proposed to extend the date for applications to 1 October before considering an increase to ten per person. Nevertheless sufficient had been taken to warrant commencement of the scheme and the committee had already started negotiations with Richard Wormald, a solicitor, for 8¼ acres of land, the very best within a reasonable distance of York.

Alderman Gray had visited the Archbishop of York who had approved of the site and promised to consecrate the chapel and the part of the ground which would be selected for the burial of members of the Church of England. The proposed cemetery was elevated and dry, composed of sand and gravel to a considerable depth, and commanded, from its undulating surface, an interesting view of the City. Five acres only were to be laid out at first with walks and plantations, combined with the trees already there, making it very ornamental and little inferior to any modern cemetery. To divert criticism of its distance from the City measurements had been made to show that it was as convenient as could possibly be expected for a cemetery outside the walls.

From		
	Micklegate Bar	1 mile 140 yds
	Monk Bar	1700 yds
	Ouse Bridge	1320 yds
	Bootham Bar	1 mile 43 yds
	Walmgate Bar	528 yds
	Foss Bridge	1087 yds

It was also thought to be possible to devise means by which the bodies of the poor and a limited number of relatives could be conveyed to the cemetery at very small expense when the distance from their homes appeared unreasonable. The committee congratulated itself that it had accomplished 'the union of so many different religious denominations in the promotion of this public object, and they cannot but hope that peace and prosperity will attend the Institution'.

To implement the plans and to superintend the management of the cemetery the provisional committee was expanded to 18 members:

The Very Revd William Cockburn
The Revd William Henry Dixon
Alderman Jonathan Gray, Solicitor a
John Robert Mills, Proctor
William Stephenson Clark, Surgeon
George Woodall, Woollen Draper a
William Napier Dibb, Solicitor a
Thomas Price, Gentleman ac
John Blanchard, Solicitor b
The Revd Charles Wellbeloved
James Pigott Pritchett, Architect ad

James Chadwick, Currier a
John Harland Fox, Tea Dealer a
Wells Hood, Wine Merchant
Benjamin Agar, Currier
Thomas Hands, Auctioneer
James Allen, Surgeon
William Slater, Solicitor b

a – members of the original provisional committee, b – solicitor & secretary, c – treasurer, d – architect

They also were given the power to co-opt additional members.[19] One member of the original provisional committee, John Clemesha, hatter, hosier and glover, was not appointed to the enlarged committee, neither did he become a shareholder of the new company.

The land, which the provisional committee had found, was part of the nursery of Thomas Rigg and Son. Thomas Rigg was born in 1746 and came to York in 1777 when he applied to the Corporation to be made a freeman as a gardener. By 1789 he was advertising setts of early potatoes in the *York Courant* which he had produced on some land in Fishergate, eventually expanded to some 45 acres mostly between Heslington Road and Fulford Barracks. His eldest son, Thomas, who had been apprenticed to his father, joined him in 1803 but died in 1811 when his second son James, came into the family business of Nurserymen and Seedsmen. On the death of James in 1833 Thomas Rigg, now aged 87, continued to run the firm with the help of his daughter-in-law, Ann, the wife of James. Tragedy seemed to dog the family of Thomas Rigg. As well as losing two sons, six of the children of James and Ann had died from childhood ailments and another six had been drowned when the boat they were in was run down on the Ouse near Acomb Landing on 19 August 1830, leaving them with only two daughters surviving from a family of 14. In the churchyard of St Lawrence a gravestone by William Plows, sculptor, with a verse by James Montgomery, the hymn writer, records the boating disaster

> Mark the brief story of a Summer's day!
> At noon, Youth, Health and Beauty launched away;
> Ere eve, death couch'd the bark and quenched their light;
> Their Parents' Home was desolate at night:'

The accident was reported throughout the country and Charles Lamb was moved to write some lines of verse about the incident.[20]

When James died in 1833 Thomas Rigg decided it was time to retire and advertised his house, 45 acres of land and his stock in trade for sale but only 21 acres were sold. He died on 12 February 1835 having directed in his will, made on 16 January and witnessed by Richard Wormald, that his remaining property was to be sold to educate his two surviving granddaughters. In October Wormald advertised that the business, now with 24 acres of land, was again for sale. The buyer of the business was the firm of Thomas and James Backhouse who, on 20 February 1836, solicited 'a continuance of the support so liberally bestowed on the firm of T. Rigg and Son during a period of so many years'. Fishergate was to become the headquarters of their business when they sold their site in Tanner Row in 1839 to the York and North Midland Railway for the new railway station. The bulk of the Rigg land, 21 acres, remained unsold so Richard Wormald arranged for it to be auctioned in nine lots at the White Swan Inn, Pavement, on 4 April. The bids made were insufficient so the lots were bought in. Two closes, which had been divided into seven lots, were lumped together and put up as a single lot. £2,000 was bid for this lot but this too was considered insufficient. In May, however, the trustees agreed to an offer of £2,200. The two closes, between Heslington Road and what was to become Cemetery Road, were almost equal in size and amounted to nearly 13 acres. The first of these Thomas Rigg had purchased in 1806 for £1,200 from William Cartwright, an innkeeper, the licensee of the Robin Hood Inn, Castlegate, and the second in 1811 for £900 from the estate of Hannah Botterill, widow of John Botterill, a grocer of Great Shambles. This offer of £2,200, only £100 greater than the original purchase price, was made, surprisingly, by a consortium of John Wilson, a surgeon, Richard Wormald and his brother, John Wormald. Richard Wormald already had a lease on part of the land and had just built some houses and outbuildings there. The partners agreed to subdivide the land amongst themselves and Richard Wormald paid £833 12s 0d for 6 acres.[21]

The Wormald brothers and John Wilson had bought this land with the intention of building streets of terraced houses for York's rapidly expanding population. In fact Bexley Square, Fitzroy Terrace, Phoenix Terrace, Phoenix Street, Walter Street and Alne Terrace were built on John Wormald's land and Whitby Terrace on John Wilson's. Richard Wormald, hearing that the cemetery committee were looking for suitable land near the City, offered his portion of the sale to them. The eventual conclusion was that an agreement was quickly reached with him to buy

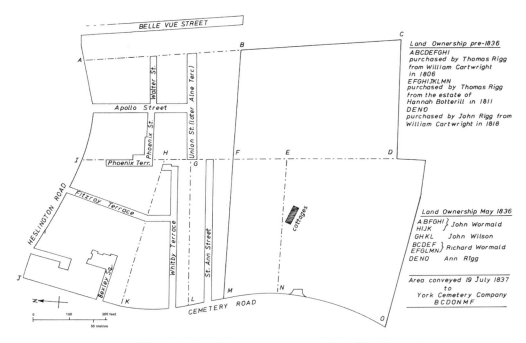

Plan 1 – York Cemetery – ownership of land

5 acres for £998, leaving him with a profit of £164 8s 0d and one acre of land on which St Ann Street was built in addition to his other houses. The remaining 3¼ acres, to make up the total purchase of 8¼ acres, was bought from Ann Rigg. Her husband had bought this land for £900 in 1818 from William Cartwright, and it was now sold for £1000. Richard Wormald was, of course, the Riggs' solicitor and had an intimate knowledge of their affairs but one wonders in whose best interest he was acting in buying land from the family and selling it for his personal gain. The cemetery committee congratulated themselves on their purchase, which also included trees and, on Ann Rigg's land, three cottages with barns and other outbuildings (estimated to be worth £200), 'for a sum [£240 an acre] which, if not cheap, is at all events not unreasonable'. It was conveyed to the cemetery trustees on 19 July 1837.[22]

The land purchased for the new cemetery had previously been a market garden made up of acquisitions in 1806, 1811 and 1818 but prior to that it been undeveloped land consisting of closes or fields, a usage of many centuries. However there is evidence for its use for burials over 1600 years previously. In 1888 Thomas

The Roman head pot found in the cemetery in 1888, now in the Yorkshire Museum

[Photograph – Hugh Murray]

Brown, then superintendent of the cemetery handed over to the Yorkshire Philosophical Society a Roman female head pot, 12 inches tall, thought to represent Julia Domna, the wife of the Emperor Septimius Severus (193-211). This must have been found by the gravediggers in the course of their duties. Pots of this sort were used either as grave goods or as funerary urns containing cremated remains but in either case the implication is that somewhere in the original 8¼ acres of the cemetery there had been at least one Roman burial. By Roman law the dead had to be buried outside the areas inhabited by the living. Burial grounds and individual grave sites were normally located alongside the approaches to settlements, in this case the road to York from the south where further evidence of a cremation cemetery was found during the construction of the Northern Command Headquarters in 1878 between Winterscale Street and Melbourne Terrace.[23]

With the land for the cemetery now secured, the committee asked their architect, James Pigott Pritchett, to prepare plans for the chapel, lodge and fences. Pritchett, born in St Petrox, Pembrokeshire, in 1789 and educated at the Royal Academy Schools in London, came to York in 1813 to work with Charles Watson. Their partnership lasted until 1831 and during this time they had been associated in such York buildings as Lendal Chapel (1816), the portico of the Assembly Rooms (1828), York County Savings' Bank (1829/30) and the Minster Song School (1830/33). After the partnership was dissolved, Pritchett continued on his own and in 1833 entered a public competition for an integrated design for the buildings, walks and general layout of a cemetery for the Leeds General Cemetery Company in Woodhouse Lane. His design, estimated to cost £6250, provided for lodges at two of the entrances (£2500 including boundary wall and gates), a chapel and vaults (£2350) at the centre of the ground, with a chaplain's house (£900) adjacent, and trenching, planting, roads and walks (£500). He also offered two cheaper versions of the chapel at £1900 and £1800. He was short-listed but failed to win the prize, allegedly because he had not provided a plan of the grave layout. More probably the combination of a local Leeds architect with a lower estimate of £5000 was an insurmountable barrier for Pritchett. He learnt of the result of the competition from the *Leeds Mercury* and immediately wrote to ask for the return of his book of plans.[24]

James Pigott Pritchett, 1789 – 1868, a founder trustee and architect of York Cemetery.

As Pritchett had already tried his hand at cemetery design and had a set of plans available, it is tempting to assume that he used the Leeds drawings for York Public Cemetery. But, whether the plans were merely re-worked to suit the York site or represented a totally new design, by November the shareholders were informed that a design and estimate (£3000) for the chapel, vaults, iron railing and wall fencing had been obtained which had received the approbation of the Archbishop, the Archdeacon and the Dean of York. By public advertisement the committee had obtained tenders and let a contract for the building work which they hoped would be completed by 1 August 1837. Being aware of the importance of having the grounds tastefully laid out the committee offered, on 5 November 1837, two premiums, a first prize of 5 guineas and a second prize of 3 guineas, to landscape gardeners for the best design for ornamenting the full 8¼ acres.[25] As 1837 drew to a close the committee of the York Public Cemetery Company, now joined by a number of shareholders, was about to see the fruition of its exertions of so many years – the attainment of a much desired object.

NOTES

1. J.C. Loudon *On the Laying Out, Planting, and Managing of Cemeteries* (1843) p 1.
2. *Report of the Commission on the Division of Counties and Boundaries of Boroughs HC* 141 (1831-2) part 6, p 171 (City of York).
3. P M. Tillot (ed.) *Victoria County History, The City of* York (1961) pp 212 and 254-8.
4. T. Laycock *Report on the State of the City of York* (1944) pp 7-8, 13-15, 26.
5. Laycock op. cit. in note 4, pp 11, 50; J. Smith *Report to the General Board of Health on a preliminary inquiry into the sewerage, drainage and supply of water, and the sanitary condition of the inhabitants of the City of York* (1850) p 28.
6. J.C. Loudon *op. cit.* in note 1, p 4.
7. A. Armstrong *Stability and Change in an English County Town* (1974) p 123.
8. M. Durey *The First Spasmodic Cholera Epidemic in York*, 1832 (1974) pp 2-8.
9. *York Courant* 16 June 1832; W Hargrove *History and Description of the Ancient City of York* (1818) Vol II p 503.
10. M. Durey *op. cit.* in note 7, pp 21-22; Royal Commission on Historical Monuments Vol III *City of York, Southwest of the Ouse* (1972) p 48a.
11. J. Smith *Report on the Condition of the City of York* (1845) p 2.
12. *Yorkshire Gazette* 20 August 1836.
13. *Yorkshire Gazette* 7 June 1834.
14. York City Archives (YCA) BB1, pp 47 & 91; BC 10/1 p 25.
15. Yorkshire Gazette 14, 28 May, 4, 11 June 1836.
16. *Norfolk Genealogy* Vol XVII Rosary Cemetery Monumental Inscriptions & Burials (n.d. [1986]) Introduction; *Eastern Daily Press* 3 May 1955.
17. J.C. Loudon *On the Laying Out, Planting, and Managing of Cemeteries* (1843, reprinted 1981) Introduction by J.S. Curl p 15.
18. *Yorkshire Gazette* 20 August 1836.
19. *Yorkshire Gazette* 9 July 1836.
20. Hugh Murray *Murray's York Pedigrees* MS at York City Reference Library; J.B. Morrell *The Biography of the Common Man of the City of York* (1947) pp 19-20 W & J. Hargrove *The New Guide for Strangers and Residents in the City of York* (1838) p 174.
21. *Yorkshire Gazette* 12 October 1833, 10 October 1835, 20 February 1836, 2 April 1836; YCA Acc 247/25.
22. YCA Acc 247/25.
23. Yorkshire Philosophical Society *A Handbook to the Antiquities in the Grounds and Museum* (1891) p. 116. Royal Commission on Historical Monuments *The City of York Vol 1, Eburacum, Roman York* (1962) p. 69
24. Leeds University, Brotherton Library, Acc 421 120/4, 161/19; R.F. Fletcher *The History of Leeds General Cemetery Company* Unpublished M. Phil thesis, (1975) pp 30, 33.
25. *Yorkshire Gazette* 19 November 1837.

2: 'Of Graves, of Worms, and Epitaphs' – Profits and Expansion

Let's talk of graves, of worms, and epitaphs;
Make dust our paper, and with rainy eyes
Write sorrow on the bosom of the earth;
Let's choose executors and talk of wills:
And yet not so – for what can we bequeath
Save our deposed bodies to the ground.

King Richard II, III, ii, 144

The first task of the provisional committee in 1837 was to get the shareholders, who had subscribed for 328 of the available 600 shares, to elect from their ranks, which included people from all walks of life, gentlemen, clerics, members of the professions, shopkeepers, tradesmen and even a cowkeeper and a labourer, trustees in whom the ownership of the land would be vested and who would set the framework of rules under which the cemetery would operate. All the members of the provisional committee were elected and, additionally,

William Oldfield, Wine Merchant
John Prest, Wholesale Druggist
The Revd John Kendrick
George Leeman, Solicitor

By the time the Deed of Settlement, giving formal status to the existence and objectives of York Public Cemetery Company, had been made on 7 March 1838, Alderman James Meek, currier, had replaced the man whose hand had guided, from the beginning, the deliberations which had led to the provision of a cemetery for York. Alderman Jonathan Gray, who had been involved in many local organisations of benefit to his fellow citizens as well as running a very busy legal practice, had served on the Board of Health during the cholera epidemic and had, immediately afterwards, become a founder member of the cemetery committee, taking the chair at its private and public meetings. He suffered from a lung complaint and it was his practice to take a recuperative autumnal tour in Scotland. After returning home in 1837, not refreshed and improved as usual, he went first

Although Jonathan Gray, the first chairman of York Cemetery Company, was buried in Hastings his family erected a monument to him, one of the first in the cemetery. Underneath a vault was constructed as a burial place for other members of his family.

[Photograph - Hugh Murray]

to Scarborough and then, on medical advice, to Hastings for the winter where he died on 11 December. He was buried there, far from home, in the churchyard of St Mary's in the Castle but is commemorated in the cemetery that he did so much to bring into being with one of its earliest and, certainly, most spectacular monuments, a gothic extravaganza, marking the Gray family vault.[1]

The Deed of Settlement declared the objectives of the cemetery company – the provision, on land to be bought with money subscribed by the shareholders, now able to hold 20 shares each, of a burial place for persons of all religious denominations. The ground, part of which was to be consecrated for Church of England burials, was to be laid out with paths, planted with shrubs and trees and enclosed by a boundary wall and fences. At the entrance a lodge was to be built and in the centre of the cemetery, a chapel. An accurate plan, showing the situation of all graves, vaults and other places of interment, was to be made and a register of all burials was to be carefully kept and preserved. The privilege of burial and purchase of graves and vaults and rights of interment, with or without religious rights, was to be open on equal terms to everybody but prompt payment was required for these privileges. Lower prices could be fixed for rights of burial and graves for the sole use of the poor, with those living in houses or tenements rated at £5 a year or less being charged only the actual cost of interment. If required purchasers of graves and vaults could have conveyances of their property. The business of the company was to be conducted by a committee of management assisted by a treasurer, clerks, chaplain, registrar, watchmen and other servants elected at an annual general meeting. The Deed of Settlement also laid down the rules of conduct of the affairs of the company and its committee.[2]

It would appear that no suitable designs for the layout of the cemetery were attracted by the offer of the premiums as a contemporary guide attributes the ground plan to Pritchett.[3] The landscaping work had started by the middle of January 1837 although the land was not legally conveyed to the cemetery company until 19 July. The Church of England had chosen the half of the ground furthest away from Cemetery Road as the portion to be consecrated, leaving the remainder for the Dissenters, and, as it was expected that burials of members of the established church would far exceed the others, it had been decided that only one acre of the Dissenters area would be used at first and the other three acres would be let out as grazing until required. When 25 year old Charlotte Hall, a Unitarian and second daughter of Thomas Fishburn Hall, a leather dresser and glove manufacturer of Clarence Street who lived at Cupola House, Heworth Moor, died on 17 January the work on the Dissenters' area, although not complete, was sufficiently advanced for her to be buried on 21 January. The service was conducted by the Revd Charles Wellbeloved and the funeral arrangements were made by Thomas Hands, both of them trustees of the cemetery company. Charlotte Hall's sad but historic role is recorded on the tombstone marking her grave between the southern perimeter path and the main drive to the chapel:

A lovely flower
removed, alas how soon
from the tender watchful care
that had reared and cherished it
to be THE FIRST transplanted
into this garden of death
yet not to continue here for ever
but at the appointed season to be taken
into the paradise of God
there to revive and flourish
in perfect and unfading beauty

The event was reported in the *Yorkshire Gazette* with the comment 'This is the first breaking of the sod to inhume a mortal's remains in the spot but how many must follow in the train is past calculation'.[4] Nearby another monument records the tragic end of a York family. Maria Slater, the infant daughter of William Slater, a cemetery trustee and secretary, was, on 19 February, the second person to be buried, followed on 15 May by her mother, Mary, the fourth burial, and finally on 26 April 1838 by William Slater himself, the 63rd burial. The York Public Cemetery Company had lost its first chairman and its first secretary in the space of five months barely had the cemetery opened.

The consecrated area sloped down from south to north and had to be levelled before the paths, in a nearly symmetrical arrangement of concentric circles within a rectangular box, could be laid out. Earth was removed from the lower area to create, at the south side of the cemetery, an elevated terrace on which the chapel was to be built. While the first specific cemetery legislation, The Cemeteries Clauses Act 1847, was to require a cemetery company to build a chapel only in the consecrated part of the ground, the trustees of York Public Cemetery Company determined that facilities should be provided for the use of Dissenters if they required them. To avoid the expense of building two chapels Pritchett designed a building that was symmetrical about its north-south axis and stood it on the dividing line between the Church of England and the Dissenters' sections. The foundation stone was laid on 4 April 1837 by James Meek, Lord Mayor of York, in the presence of the few spectators, including Jonathan Gray, who had braved the inclement November-like weather. The Lord Mayor's remarks, 'in a brief but excellent address', expressing gratification that the promoters of the undertaking had provided a very much needed cemetery 'that would be hailed with pleasure by the inhabitants of this city in consequence of the present crowded state of their churchyards', must have produced the invitation to him, made after the death of Jonathan Gray, to become a trustee.[5]

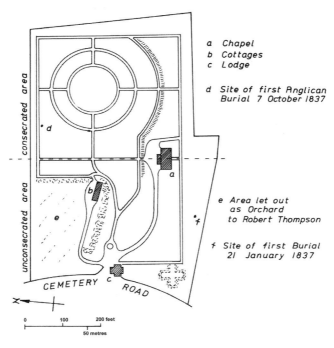

Plan 2 – York Cemetery 1837–47

Pritchett's design for the chapel, a late flowering of the Greek Revival style with its pagan connotations which was about to be replaced in English cemeteries by the more religiously respectable Gothic fashion, is based on the temple of Erectheus in Athens and constructed in white stone from Roche Abbey. Internally it measures 58 feet 4 inches by 25 feet and could hold a congregation of 300 people who, in 1837, on entering the bald, bare and unheated interior through the Ionic portico, would have sat on straight high backed pews behind the curtained box pews that hid the mourners from their sight. Two box pulpits on stilts were provided; one at each end, for the officiating clergymen and in the centre was a large sarcophagus, on which the coffin rested during the service. If the coffin was to be interred in the arched vaults below the chapel, the middle part of the sarcophagus could be slowly and solemnly lowered by concealed machinery, possibly of the type invented by Mr Smith, Engineer, of Princes Street, Leicester Square, and installed at Kensal Green Cemetery for £400. Other vaults, less highly priced, were provided under the steps of the portico.[6]

It had been hoped that all the buildings would be completed by 1 August but, in early September, with the grounds ready for use and the chapel still unfinished, it was decided to invite Edward Venables Vernon Harcourt, Archbishop of York, to consecrate the parts of the chapel and burial ground to be used by the Church of England. The Archbishop's diary, at this time, does not seem to have been filled with many, if any, engagements as he agreed to perform the 'rare and interesting ceremony' on Thursday 14 September at 12 o'clock, or if it was raining on that day, at the same hour on the first fine day afterwards[7]: As it turned out this was a wise precaution. It rained on the first appointed day but the next day the weather was favourable so the Archbishop proceeded to the cemetery where, awaiting his arrival, were 2,000 people of the 'more respectable classes` with a large proportion of ladies – 'a gay and lively throng, scarcely calculated to remind the spectator of the solemn purpose to which the scene is to be devoted, yet perfectly in keeping with the cheerful looking garden into which the place has been converted'. As the chapel was not ready, a tent, part of the arrangements for the event made by James Pigott Pritchett, had been erected alongside it to shelter the aged Archbishop and the supporting clergy during the ceremony. This included a declaration that the ground was to be separated from all profane and common uses and assigned for the burial of the dead according to the rites of the Church of England as by law established. The ceremony over, the spectators wandered round the broad gravel paths between the smooth lawns relieved by flower beds and incipient shrubs and trees arranged on the 'principles of landscape gardening'.[8]

'An engraving of the lodge, the chapel, and the pallisadoes as they appear from the road' as represented in Hargrove's New Guide for Strangers and Residents in 1838.

The original entrance gates, supplied by the Walker Iron Foundry and illustrated in its pattern book, were replaced by the present gates in 1880. The portico of the lodge was filled in as an office in 1861 and removed in 1892 when a larger office, extending to the nearest gate pillar, was constructed.

[Photograph by courtesy of York Castle Museum, Department of Leisure Services, York City Council]

Facing Cemetery Road the grounds are enclosed by a low stone wall surmounted by iron railings supported at intervals by stone pillars; the terminal pillar at the north end being crowned by a sarcophagus and the one at the other extremity by a sphinx. The central pillars, ornamented with urns, supported elaborate gates, a double one in the centre for carriages and single gates on either side for pedestrians. All the iron work was from John Walker's iron foundry in Walmgate.[9] The lodge, again in Greek Revival style, for the chaplain and John Shields, the resident gardener and cemetery superintendent, at the south side of the gates had, before more recent extensions at both front and rear, a simple portico facing the entrance drive. Pritchett's design for the two cemetery buildings, the chapel and lodge, and the railings and gate make a harmonious ensemble and cost the company, with the laying out of the grounds, just short of £4,400 in addition to £1,998 paid for the land. The sale of shares had only realised £3,280 so the first annual general meeting on 20 July 1838 agreed that at least another 160 shares should be sold, the existing shareholders having preference up to the limit of 20 each. The additional £1,600 together with £1,500 borrowed from Ann Rigg

The pallisaded iron fence along Cemetery Road, also supplied by the Walker Iron Foundry, terminates at a large stone pillar at each end - one surmounted with a sphinx, and the other at the north end, with a sarcophagus, both symbolic of death.

[Photograph - Helen Kirk]

at 3.9%, presumably most of the proceeds of the sale of her and her father-in-law's land, would enable the company to clear its debts with the City and County Bank.[10] The eventual consequence for James Pigott Pritchett from this first success was that 17 years later his firm, Pritchett & Sons of York and Darlington, was to establish a national reputation as cemetery designers, being responsible for cemeteries at Boston (1854), Tottenham (1855), Mansfield and Scarborough (1856), Darlington (1857) Colne, Lancashire (1859), Whitby (1861), and Great Driffield (1864) before his death in 1868.[11]

With the Archbishop's duties performed, the Church of England section of the cemetery was ready for use but it was not until 7 October that a burial was made in consecrated ground. This was the body of William Nicholson, a 29 year old servant from Garden Place, Hungate, who had died of typhus four days previously. As the chapel was still not complete the Revd Isaac Grayson, curate of Holy Trinity, King's Court, had to perform the service in a temporary building adjoining it, before the body was laid to rest in a public grave in the centre of the south side of the consecrated area. It had been dug to a depth of 14 feet in dry sandy gravel and seven more bodies were placed in it over the next two months before it was finally filled. Nicholson's family paid 4s 6d for the burial, which included the minister's fee, with another 3s 0d for his body and eight mourners to be conveyed to the cemetery in a special hearse provided by the company for the convenience of the poor who lived at a distance.[12] This vehicle had already been noticed at the consecration service when it was described as 'a large lugubrious black vehicle with glazed black curtains' which from its 'commodious dimensions' was conjectured to be 'a sort of economic utilitarian combination of hearse and mourning coach'. It would seem that York Public Cemetery Company was right at the forefront of funeral technology as it was only in June that year that J.R. Croft of Bayswater had suggested that the expense of funerals could be reduced by the adoption of a double-bodied omnibus hearse of his design with a tight partition between the corpse and mourners to prevent offensive smells reaching them.[13]

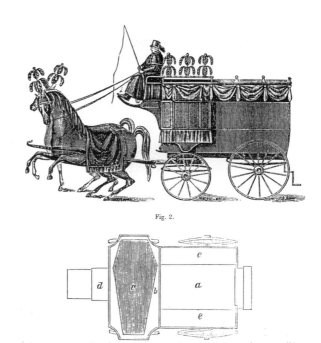

Fig. 2.

A combined mourning coach and hearse invented by J.R. Croft of Bayswater in 1837. This is similar to the one seen in York Cemetery at the consecration service in September of the same year.

Although the company had enshrined in the Deed of Settlement the right of a parish priest to perform the burial rites for his parishioners in the cemetery, it had great difficulty in persuading the clergy of York to do so. A letter had been addressed to each of them asking if they would be willing to avail themselves of the liberty of officiating at their parishioners' funerals. This met with no success presumably because the incumbent's income would be reduced if members of their flock were encouraged to forgo the right of burials in their own churchyard however crowded and unsanitary it was. The only solution was the appointment of a regular cemetery chaplain. The first was the Revd J.H. Newton, who as a curate (of St Dennis's), would have had little to sacrifice by the loss of parish fees and, except for the inconvenience of being available every day, everything to gain. He commenced his additional duties on 24 October 1837, for a fee of 2s 0d per interment, but left York in May 1838, to be replaced by the Revd Robert Sutton, vicar of St Oswald's, Fulford, who was in no danger of losing his fees for burials in his own churchyard and could only benefit by accepting the vacant post. It was said that he had only agreed to take it until a successor to Newton was found but he held the post for just over five years when the Revd Josiah Crofts, rector of St Saviours', was appointed.[14]

When the shareholders met at the first annual general meeting in the Guildhall on 20 July 1838 they heard from John Blanchard that, up to 25 June, there had been 87 burials in the cemetery since it opened, 62 in the consecrated and 25 in the unconsecrated sections. On the other hand during the same period the number of burials in York would have been about 1000. It appeared that the citizens of York were reluctant to forgo their right of burial in their own parish graveyard but the committee of management were not downhearted and, in spite of having to pay interest on loans, recommended a dividend of 4%. The secretary's report concluded by congratulating the subscribers: -

> on the full accomplishment of the object for which this institution was established, viz., to provide for the inhabitants of this city and vicinity, the means of decent and undisturbed sepulture, according to the rites of their own religious faith; and your committee have been gratified at the repeated testimonials of their fellow-citizens, not only as to the beauty and excellence of the general arrangement of the buildings and the grounds, but also of the solemn and decorous manner in which the funerals have been conducted, and the attention paid to the keeping in order, and planting the earth, which covers the remains of their beloved relatives.

The prospects for the cemetery were thought to be highly encouraging and the public benefits it conferred were becoming daily more obvious and appreciated. Everything in the garden [of death] was lovely![15]

As well as providing the means of a decent and undisturbed burial, the cemetery was planted out with shrubs, in borders of various forms, including, to the right of the entrance, a cross shape, which when fully grown would 'constitute a solemn shade over the recess representing this sacred emblem'. It was said to form one of the most interesting walks in the neighbourhood, thereby fulfilling Loudon's secondary objective for a burial ground – 'the improvement of the moral sentiments and general taste of all classes, and more especially of the great masses of society'. Thus having begun the process of the removal of a nuisance, the miasma produced by decomposing bodies, from the crowded dwellings in the City, the citizens were being encouraged to enjoy walks among it. The difference, however, would have been startling in these early days; the effect of a few bodies interred at a proper depth in an eight-acre cemetery would hardly have been noticeable. The grounds were freely open to the public, except on Sundays, but the hospitality of the cemetery company was frequently abused by those who picked the fruit and flowers and even stole the plants out of the ground. The cemetery staff who were on duty at opening times were encouraged to be more vigilant but when the cemetery was closed it was said to be effectively guarded, with the help, until 1870, of a watchdog at the lodge. This must have provided a suitable and cheap deterrent; its keep never exceeded £2 12s 0d a year and was usually much less. Its main function, however, must have been to keep away the resurrection men.[16]

It was a criticism to be made against the York Cemetery Company that its charges were excessive[17] and, certainly, this can be seen in the price of burial in a private grave where the example followed seems to have been that of the Leeds General Cemetery opened at Woodhouse Moor in 1835. For vaults in the open cemetery and the burial of the poor York Public Cemetery Company led the field for cheapness.[18] Nevertheless the gentry, professional people and employers of York, members of the higher social strata, were not deterred and led the move away from parish burial. In the first three years after the opening of the cemetery the interments in public graves were three quarters of the total but the artisan and unskilled classes amounted to nearly four fifths of the population of the City. By the 1850s the proportions matched exactly.[19] Even amongst the higher orders class distinction was apparent, with three vaults being constructed in the open ground and four burials being made in the slightly cheaper (£8 10s 0d including a black marble inscribed slab) catacombs under the chapel. John Gowland, an Officer of the Excise from Heworth, was the first to be placed, in a special coffin, on a shelf in the catacombs. His funeral was held on 3 February 1838, the first indication that the chapel was complete. When Edward Prest, a gentleman of Blossom Street and a shareholder of the cemetery company, was interred in the catacombs on 4 September 1839, two of his children, Edward, died December 1832, and Matilda, died November 1834, previously buried in the churchyard of St Mary Bishophill Junior, were exhumed to join him. Cheap as this method of disposal was, it was not popular, probably because of the cost of the coffin required, a glass tank, in which the body was preserved in formalin, contained in an oak coffin and then sealed into a sheet metal box. Only 17 people, including the two Prest children, were stored away in this way to await the last trump.

Figure i *Comparative Charges - Private Graves*

Cemetery Company	Size of Plot	Cost of Grave plot	Charge for 1st burial	Total
York	7½ft x 3ft	£3 15s 0d	15s 0d	£4 10s 0d
Leeds				
General W	7ft x 3½ft	£3 15s 0d	17s 6d	£4 12s 6d
E	7ft x 3½ft	£3 0s 0d	17s 6d	£3 17s 6d
Liverpool				
Low Mill		£3 0s 0d	17s 6d	£3 17s 6d
Kirkdale		£3 0s 0d	17s 6d	£3 17s 6d
Manchester				
Rusholme Rd		£2 14s 6d		
Sheffield				
General		£2 12s 6d	17s 6d	£3 10s 0d
Kensal Green				
All Souls	6ft x 2½ft	£3 3s 0d	£2 2s 0d	£5 5s 0d

Figure ii *Comparative Charges - Public Graves (Poor Burial) and Vaults*

Cemetery Company	Public Grave (Poor Burial) Total Cost	Cost of Vault	Charge for 1st burial	Total Cost of burial
York	4s 6d*	£9 0s 0d	£1 0s 0d	£10 0s 0d
Leeds				
General W	5s 0d	£9 15s 0d	£1 2s 0d	£10 17s 6d
E	10s 0d	£9 0s 0d	£1 2s 0d	£10 0s 0d
Liverpool				
Low Mill	10s 0d	£9 0s 0d	£1 2s 0d	£10 2s 0d
Kirkdale	10s 0d	£9 0s 0d	£1 2s 0d	£10 2s 0d
Manchester				
Rusholme Rd	8s 0d	£12 0s 0d	£1 0s 0d	£13 0s 0d
Sheffield				
General	8s 0d	£10 10s 0d	£1 2s 0d	£11 12s 0d
Kensal Green				
All Souls	25s 0d	£15 0s 0d	£26 5s 0d	£41 5s 0d

*This was the actual cost of the burial. Other users of public graves were charged 10s 6d, allowing a profit of 6s 0d for the company.

In the first sixteen years of its existence the cemetery company employed just one sexton for grave digging, initially at a weekly wage of 15s 0d, increased to 17s 0d in July 1845. At times, however, when there were more burials than he could cope with, self-employed workers were used who were generally paid 6d for each foot excavated. In 1854, just before the closure of all the City graveyards, an extra sexton was employed, and then in 1855, with the number of burials starting to rise, a third joined the staff. The same pattern was repeated in the stone-yard where the weekly wage was, at first £1 0s 0d, increasing to £1 4s 0d in July 1845.

The working class, perhaps, had more reason to be slower in accepting the facilities offered in the new cemetery. In forgoing the right of burial in the parish graveyard, not only would the relatives of the deceased have to pay for a more costly funeral but also the body would have to share a public grave with strangers, who, in the unconsecrated section, could be of a different denomination. In the consecrated section the first public grave, dug to 14 feet, contained, when filled, 8 bodies. In February 1838 A. Severs, the gravedigger, was paid 8s 6d for digging a public grave 19½ feet deep. This was certainly necessary as the average occupancy of public graves in the consecrated area in 1838 was 13. At the end of 1838 the Cemetery Company must have realised that the 7½ft x 3ft grave could be more efficiently, and profitably, used and had increased the occupancy to 18 but, not content with that, by June 1839 were putting 24 bodies in a public grave, taking at least two months to fill it. Usually only some six to eight of the bodies were adults: the remainder, in those days of high infant mortality, were young children. Even in death the poor were as closely packed together as they had been in life. It was better to be a Dissident as then one only had to share one's last resting place with, on average, five others. To get so many bodies in one grave it is possible that they were not buried in coffins. They could have been taken to the cemetery in a parish coffin, which was then emptied into the grave, collapsed like a flat-pack and returned to the church for the next occasion. Alternatively a cheap coffin, costing as little as 3s 6d, which had no handles or name plate could have been used and, as it was made without nails, often collapsed on its way to the grave side.[20] Once in the grave it certainly would have, thereby saving space.

The public graves were 'indiscriminately' placed among the private graves and family vaults and not relegated to the least valuable parts of the cemetery. Once filled they were closed, planted over and marked on the ground plan as graves never to be opened again, something which could not be realised in the City churchyards. The York Public Cemetery Company congratulated itself on this policy which it thought was one of the reasons why it was approved of so greatly by the poor. But having shown itself to be practising an enlightened regime of no class distinction in death, the company then went on to give the real reason for its policy:

This is advantageous to the latter [private graves] for as monuments are very seldom placed on public graves open space is thus secured round the Tombs, which would otherwise be crowded together more frequently than at present.

Enlightenment, after all, was designed to allow the wealthy to continue, after death, the privileges they had enjoyed in life but there had to be some benefit to the cemetery company. At first poor burials accounted for half the interments in the cemetery but by 1853 had risen to two thirds and, as the charge of 4s 6d only covered the actual expenses incurred, the company needed to be able to offer some incentive to attract the better off and the profits that would accrue from them.[21]

A new concept of a second class grave for six bodies was launched in 1848 for those families not wishing to suffer the indignity of an ordinary public grave but who did not require or could not afford the privilege of a private grave. This was really another form of public grave but for £1 15s 0d a family was able to purchase an identifiable if not private last resting place for a loved one. This fee included up to six lines of inscription on the ledger stone which eventually covered the grave. These graves could not, however, be reserved for future use by the same family.[22]

Those who required a vault in the open cemetery or under the colonnades or the portico of the chapel, where interments could be made in ordinary wooden coffins, could bring in their own workmen for its construction. While they could perhaps make the vault more cheaply than the cemetery company's staff, they had to observe its regulations or risk being removed from the ground. Purchasers of graves could employ any stonemason to make and erect a monument and here the company reserved the right to 'exclude every thing manifestly objectionable'. Alternatively the cemetery company had their own stonemasons and would provide a flat gravestone from between £1 10s 0d and £2 0s 0d on which the inscription would be carved with head letters at 3s 0d a dozen, capitals at 2s 0d and small letters at 1s 0d. For a footstone, in addition, an extra 8s 0d was required. The cemetery stone-yard and workshops were housed in the cottages and outbuildings that were on the land bought from Ann Rigg. One cottage and the land not at first required for the burial of Dissidents were let to Robert Thompson for an annual rent of £15 4s 0d.[23]

Robert Thompson had bought from Richard Wormald the remainder of his purchase from the Rigg estate which lay to the north of the cemetery and in 1843 reached an agreement to sell a small portion of it to the company for £100. Here

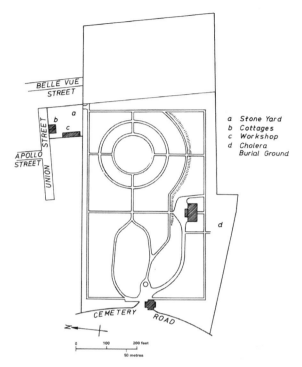

BELLE VUE STREET

APOLLO STREET

STREET

UNION

a   Stone Yard
b   Cottages
c   Workshop
d   Cholera
    Burial Ground

a

b

c

d

CEMETERY ROAD

N

0   100   200 feet

50 metres

Plan 3 – York Cemetery 1847–57

it was proposed to build new cottages and workshops whenever it was thought necessary to lay out the remainder of the unconsecrated ground. Thompson, no doubt realising that it could be more profitably used for speculative housing, subsequently went back on his agreement and left the company with a problem which was not solved until 1847 when John Wormald offered to sell 1376 square yards of land between the north wall of the cemetery and Union Street (later to be called Alne Terrace) with good access from Heslington Road. This too came from the Rigg estate and John Wormald was just about to commence building several terraces there. The price the cemetery company paid was £150, equivalent to £528 an acre, a considerable increase on £200 an acre which Wormald had paid for it but its value had been enhanced by his building plans. The land was conveyed to the cemetery company on 9 September and, at the annual general meeting in June 1848, the shareholders were informed that the old cottages had been pulled down, the orchard laid out as a cemetery and two new cottages and a workshop had been built round a stone-yard on the new land. The conveyancing and architect's fees together with the building work had cost £428 1s 7d. To cover all the costs it was proposed to raise £500 by issuing 50 unsold shares and defray the remaining £78 1s 7d out of profits.[24]

With 8¼ acres the York Public Cemetery Company had, it calculated, enough land to meet the burial needs of the City for at least 90 years. The cemetery was marked out with grave plots measuring 7½ft x 3ft providing 15,571 spaces. If, as the company assumed, each was to take five bodies, an average that took into account the ratio of public to private graves and their relative occupancy, and the mortality rate was 1000 deaths a year, the figure was actually 75 years but the shareholders at the 1847 annual general meeting probably were not concerned with checking the arithmetic, having just been offered a dividend of 5%, double that of the previous year.[25] With this rosy view of the future the company was not seeking to increase its size but Samuel Tuke, who owned Howland Close adjoining the east end of the cemetery, wanted to sell his land. Several people were interested and one had actually taken an option to buy but later decided not to complete the purchase. When this deal fell through, the cemetery company, knowing that the land was never likely to come on the market again, decided to borrow money from the York City & County Bank to purchase it. The security offered and accepted for this loan was the new land itself and that previously bought from Richard Wormald.

On 16 October 1848, for £888 18s 6d (£300 an acre), the company gained nearly three acres which brought the size of the cemetery up to 11 acres, nearly double the area of all the 24 churchyards in the City centre. The capacity of the cemetery had been increased by an extra 5,559 grave spaces. Using the same assumptions as previously, the company now calculated, correctly, that the cemetery would be 'adequate to the wants of York for 100 years to come *without disturbing the remains of any individual interred therein.*' It was, of course, an invariable rule of the company that no grave would ever be reopened and it would seem unnecessary to have added the last words to the statement unless it was having second thoughts. Burials in the consecrated section were, as had been expected, exceeding those in the unconsecrated by a ratio of three to one and it was useful to have this additional land adjacent to the consecrated section but, as it was not wanted immediately, the tenant, Joseph Walker, a publican of Walmgate, was allowed to continue using it for pasture at a rent of £15 a year, with six months notice to be given to him when the land was required by the company.[26] His tenancy was somewhat disturbed in 1851 when, in one corner of the new field, a valuable bed of gravel and stones was found which would provide a permanent supply of material for the roads and walks in the cemetery. The gravel required would otherwise have cost £40 and, although the labour charge to extract it was £15 8s 0d, it was hoped to recover this by selling the larger stones to the Road Commissioners. The hole produced by the excavation provided a place where surplus earth from the newly dug graves could be deposited. This was always a problem in cemeteries, especially if it came from a consecrated section. Consecrated soil could neither be sold nor removed from the cemetery, a difficulty eventually solved by legislation, and raised the level of the cemetery unevenly if spread round a newly dug grave.[27]

York suffered another cholera epidemic in 1849. Although not quite as severe in York as the 1832 epidemic there were 155 deaths from this disease between 9 July and 16 October, which started in Friargate and finished in nearby Middle Water Lane, both crowded and poor areas of the City. But as usual the disease found its way into the homes of the better off. During the first epidemic a special burial ground, outside the walls, had been provided by the corporation of York for that and future outbreaks but in 1849, with York cemetery well established, there was no need to reopen that graveyard. An unused area behind the chapel on the southern boundary of the cemetery was set aside and 147 of the victims were buried there in 30 public graves. The average of five bodies a grave was well down on the cemetery company's desired maximum but undoubtedly the characteristics of the disease required the graves to be closed quickly. With most of the victims safely segregated away from the rest of the cemetery, class distinction was perpetuated for eight members of well-to-do families. Their bodies were interred in family graves and vaults.[28]

John Shields, the first superintendent of the cemetery and clerk to the company, left York in 1846, presumably to go to another cemetery elsewhere, as in 1854 he was appointed to the post of superintendent of the newly incorporated Hull General Cemetery. The advertisement for his replacement in York attracted 15 applicants which the committee reduced to a short list of two – William Powell Ruddock from Easingwold and a Mr Blair, an employee of James Backhouse and Son in their nurseries in York, who had been gardener to Lord Howden. At the annual general meeting on 7 August Ruddock was elected to the vacancy and the cemetery gained an employee who brought enthusiasm and energy to all aspects of his work. A year later the committee reported that he had `discharged the duties of his office with efficiency and to the entire satisfaction of the committee'.

He continued to earn such laudatory remarks in subsequent years. In 1848 the attention of the shareholders was drawn to the state of the grounds 'which are highly creditable to Mr. Ruddock's ability and industry; and which increasingly attract the notice and the visits of the citizens and visitors of York'.[29]

John Shields had received a salary of £52 10s 0d but Ruddock was paid £60 0s 0d a year when he became superintendent and was recommended for an increase of £10 a year in 1852. In that year the first Register of Burials had been filled with 5,380 entries and had proved to be more valuable than anticipated. Frequent applications for certificates of burial were made by the Bank of England and other companies and Ruddock had made an alphabetical index to make searches easier. The Register had been kept in a fireproof closet at the cemetery lodge but, because of its value, the committee thought a duplicate should be made and deposited at the City and County Bank. Ruddock had undertaken to make this copy and, also, send the bank copies of the entries every three months. The reward for this considerable addition to his work load was a bonus of £10. His salary was used, on one occasion, to enhance the beauty of the grounds. On 13 May 1858 his 20 year old daughter, Sarah, planted in the north east corner of the cemetery a *Wellingtonea Gigantia* which he had bought from Backhouses for £1 0s 0d. 'Long may it flourish' he wrote in the Register but, sad to say, this early import of that species into England no longer survives.[30]

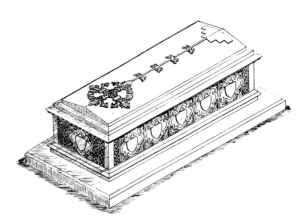

This chest tomb, drawn by W.P. Ruddock in his pattern book which he used when selling monuments to bereaved relatives, was designed by A.H. Cates, a York architect, for John Clifton, gentleman of Micklegate. It was constructed in the cemetery stone-yard and can still be seen in the Roman Catholic section west of the chapel.

Ruddock's prime enthusiasm, perhaps, was directed at the provision of a high standard of tombs and memorials to grace the grounds under his care. He visited other cemeteries and graveyards; Glasgow Necropolis; Woodhouse Cemetery, Leeds; Tintern Abbey; Caerwent churchyard, Monmouthshire; Emley churchyard, West Riding; Hull General Cemetery; Highgate Cemetery; Newcastle Cemetery; Whitby churchyard. He drew the monuments which caught his eye in those places, as good examples of their kind, in a sketch book into which he also pasted samples of lettering and decoration culled from books and other sources. Those monuments which he thought suitable for York cemetery he redrew, showing great skill as a draughtsman, with others designed by himself and a number of architects, into a pattern book that could be shown to the owners of private graves when they were considering what memorial to erect for their departed relatives. Several choices of stone were offered, from Huddlestone, Anston and Park Spring, with the cemetery stone-yard price concealed by a letter code. A number of these monuments can still be found in the cemetery but others, usually the most spectacular, have since disappeared. William Powell Ruddock died on 26 April 1861 from tuberculosis at the early age of 46 and was buried on 1 May in the consecrated section of his cemetery where a headstone, provided by his employers, marks the last resting place of its 'much and deservedly respected' servant of 15 years. Shortly after his death James Pigott Pritchett purchased the sketch book from Mrs Ruddock for the company. [31]

The classical monument to Henry Robinson, made in the cemetery stone-yard no longer exists. In his pattern book W.P. Ruddock offered it to other customers for £98.

While Ruddock was superintendent the cemetery company realised the prosperity that its shareholders wanted and it started to pay steady and reliable dividends, not only because of his efficiency, energy and enthusiasm but also from a major national reform in December 1854. In 1846 one third of the persons dying in York were buried in the cemetery, increasing the next year to a half and thereafter only very slowly but after 1854 the cemetery company got virtually all York's dead for burial. Before then the remainder of the bodies were buried in the overcrowded and insanitary churchyards in the centre of York; the right of the deceased to be buried (more cheaply than in the new cemetery) by his parish priest in his parish churchyard with his ancestors was still being exercised despite a large and growing feeling against the practice.

The York Health of Towns Association had been formed in September 1846 by some of the City's most socially concerned citizens and met regularly as a pressure group for public health reform. On 10 June 1847 the Association was addressed by Alfred Ely Hargrove, proprietor of the *York Herald*, at a meeting in the Merchants' Hall, on *The Baneful Custom of Interment in Towns and the Present State of York Graveyards*. He detailed the sorry state of the churchyards, for example, St Sampson's

> contains about 30 perches, and is in such a disgusting state that no interments can take place without interfering with human remains. In some parts, too, it is so *wet and swampy* that graves have been known to be partly filled with water, prior to the interment taking place; and when the coffin has been lowered, it has plunged out of sight, into a mass of loathsome mire, whilst the mourners have *shuddered* around.

Some of the strange scenes he had seen were described:

> In opening a grave in one of the churchyards, a considerable quantity of bones were exhumed, some of them with *fragments of flesh* still adhering. A hungry dog entered the sacred ground, seized a leg bone in his mouth and bore it away in triumph to his lair, where he doubtless would *feast* on the putrefying remnants of mortality. The bone which I hold in my hand, a portion of a skull, was rescued from a group of children, in Walmgate, who had become possessed of the greater portion of a skeleton, with which they were amusing themselves.

He concluded by reciting the 'indubitable evidence' of the way noxious matter from the churchyards affected the health of the citizens by diffusing into the air, passing through the sewers and polluting the water of wells.[32]

Soon afterwards, on 14 July, as a result of a well supported petition, the Lord Mayor of York, George Hudson, called a public meeting in the Guildhall at which many influential citizens aired the problem and passed a number of resolutions. Dr Goldie made the general proposition 'that the interment of the dead in towns is injurious to the health of the inhabitants, and that the practice thereof ought to be entirely discontinued' while Samuel Tuke, who believed that the living ought to have a respect for the remains of the dead, proposed, more specifically, 'that the crowded state of the graveyards in this city is such, that further interments therein will be extremely injurious to the health of the citizens, and can only be effected by an indecent desecration of the remains of the dead'. A suggested solution was for the parishes to have extra-mural graveyards but, as a bill was soon to be introduced in Parliament for the health of towns, nothing concrete was done to alleviate the immediate problem in York. Hudson, Member of Parliament for Sunderland, was asked 'to apply that vigorous intellect by which he had been enabled to carry out so many grand undertakings' to find a solution.[33]

Six years were to elapse before any positive steps were taken to close the City centre graveyards. In 1853 the corporation sent a circular to the authority responsible for each burial ground, asking if interments were still continuing to take place there, was it considered to be crowded, were there burial vaults in the church and was there any objection to the burial ground being closed. Of the 24 parish burial grounds in the City 13 had been closed, 5 were partially closed, one, though crowded, was still being used and five were not considered to be crowded, including St Olave's, where the incumbent, the Revd Frederick Bartlett, had every objection to the closure as it would break the tie between the people and their pastor and, perhaps more importantly, reduce his already small income. The burial grounds belonging to the Non-conformist churches were occasionally, but rarely, being used. This was certainly a great improvement but the closures that had been made were voluntary.

The corporation decided, after hearing the results of the survey at its meeting on 30 May, to petition Parliament to pass a measure to allow municipal corporations the power to purchase land 'for the purpose of public sepulture'. This was provided in the Burial Act 1854 but the Burial Act 1853 had already given the Home Secretary the power to close all existing burial grounds in large towns, a right which Lord Palmerston was 'fully and irrevocably' determined to exercise. After learning this from the Home Secretary's representative, Dr Sutherland, who had visited York on 1 July 1854, the Lord Mayor, George Leeman, told the Council that when the graveyards had been properly and legally closed, they could if they wished, appoint a burial board to provide alternative facilities but he believed there was no necessity for this as York had a cemetery which was capable of fully answering the purposes of the City; as well he might as a founder trustee of York Public Cemetery Company! Alderman R.H. Anderson doubted the wisdom of the City being placed at 'the mercy of a trading burial company' and thought it better to open more public and less expensive cemeteries. Alderman James Meek, another cemetery company trustee, came to the defence of the Lord Mayor and, after recognising that his opinion might be seen to be governed by interested motives, defended the cemetery company against animadversion; 'it buried the poor at prime cost – (laughter) – and if they had a burial ground for each ward ...... the expense of interments would be greatly increased'.[34]

Lord Palmerston caused a notice to be posted on all York churches on 29 October, informing the parishioners that, for the public health, he had made a representation to Queen Victoria that all burials should cease, from a date to be determined, in the churches, and churchyards of York, as well as the three Non-conformist burial grounds, and no new cemetery should be opened in York or within two miles of its boundary without his permission. Intermural burials in All Saints, Pavement, were, unaccountably, omitted from the list. The Privy Council met on 1 December and the Queen signed an Order in Council on 11 December bringing the prohibition into effect on 23 December 1854, followed by another on 9 February 1855 to cover the omission of All Saints, Pavement.[35] The cemetery company did not yet have a clear field for itself. The council still had to decide if the cemetery could meet the needs of the City and, on 16 January, the Urban Sanitary Committee directed the Town Clerk and the City Surveyor to make enquiries. Four days later James Pigott Pritchett replied with the information that there were still 12,594 unoccupied graves in the original 8½ acres and the average occupancy was expected to be 6½. If the mortality rate was 1,200 a year then there was sufficient room for more than 60 years. Additionally the price of 4s 6d for the burial of the poor, more than half of the total interments, was the average of that in the old churchyards. On hearing this at its meeting on 12 February the committee merely directed that Pritchett's letter be entered in the minutes; by this formula they tacitly accepted that the York Public Cemetery Company could and should have the monopoly of burying the City's dead.

The cemetery company, however, still had a problem. The field bought from Samuel Tuke to extend its grounds had been excluded from the information given to the corporation because there was some doubt if the London Burial Board would allow it to be used. Since it had been acquired, some houses had been built in the adjacent field and the Cemeteries Clauses Act 1847 prescribed that no cemetery should be constructed within 200 yards of any house without the consent in writing of its owner, lessee and occupier. Worse, the London Burial Board were currently thinking that only one body should be buried in each grave and then, after 15 years, be dug up to make room for others![36] An Inspector of Burial Grounds was sent to York on 19 December 1856 and he was prepared to recommend to the Home Secretary that consent be given to the use of the new field on condition only that the regulations of the London Burial Board were observed. No mention was made of the proximity of the new houses. The London Burial Board had relaxed its ideas on grave occupancy slightly. A grave could be reopened whenever a death occurred in the same family, but it now laid down that the grave plots should be 9ft x 4ft; at one fell swoop the number of grave spaces was reduced from 5,559 to 2,832, a small disaster that was to be ameliorated by charging £5 5s 0d for the enlarged grave space instead of £3 15s 0d, the charge for a plot in the original area of the cemetery. With permission granted the laying out of the walks, graves and drainage, estimated to cost £200, was started and Thomas Musgrave, Archbishop of York, was invited to consecrate it on 14 Aug 1857.[37] When the day came the weather was inclement and there was only a scanty attendance. The Archbishop robed in the chapel and then made a circuit of the new ground, reciting, alternatively with the people present, the verses of the 49th psalm, a reminder that wealth was of no use after death when low and high, rich and poor were all equal. 'His Grace then offered up, in an impressive manner, the usual consecration prayer, and dismissed the congregation with the Benediction.'[38] The first burial in the new ground was made on 7 September 1858 but it was only used infrequently at first, perhaps because of the increased fees for graves in this area. An attempt in 1865 by James Meek to reduce the charge by a guinea to £4 4s 0d was strongly opposed by Michael Charlton who was able to rally sufficient support to defeat the proposal.[39]

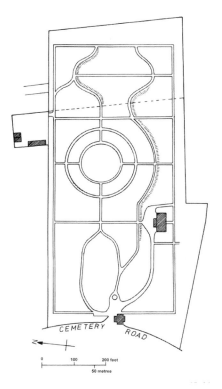

Plan 4 – York Cemetery 1857–68

Up to the year immediately preceding the closure of the City graveyards the number of burials in the cemetery had never exceeded 601 in a year but in 1854 it rose to 760, with 892 in the next year. The 1000 barrier was exceeded for the first time in 1858. The cemetery was now realising its potential but a new problem was soon apparent. A CITIZEN, writing to the *Yorkshire Herald* on 9 February 1856, drew attention to the 'deleterious effect coming from the present crowded cemetery in Fulford Road'. 'The cemetery', he went on to say, 'used to be thought a beautiful and retired spot, where the mourner could frequent its pleasant walks, and look with sweet consolation on the tranquil grave of some loved one. Now, alas, all this is passing quickly away, and the offensive odour in warm weather makes one hurry forward'. The cemetery superintendent, however, was already using McDougall's Disinfecting Powder to alleviate what otherwise would have been an intolerable problem.[40] There was one consolation, however, for the company. The original area of the cemetery, already naturally well drained, could never get into the sorry state that had existed in some of the City centre churchyards but, nevertheless, in 1853 the Corporation had asked for a contribution of £50 towards the estimated cost of £350 for a sewer, 650 yards long, to be laid from Cemetery Road to the River Ouse near New Walk Terrace. At the annual general meeting on 22 Aug 1854, James Pigott Pritchett gave his opinion that this drain, to be laid 14 feet below the road surface, could only improve the property but the meeting did not agree with him. The Corporation renewed its demand for £50 in September but, again, apparently without result, as the company, perhaps with the immediate prospect of extending its land into a less well drained area of nearly 5½ acres belonging to George Wilson, asked in August 1867 the terms on which it would be allowed to lay a drain to the now constructed common sewer in Elmwood Street. It was told that it must lay the drain at its own expense and pay a yearly acknowledgement of £1 to the Corporation.[41]

Thus, when William Powell Ruddock died in 1861, all the aims of the York Public Cemetery Company were realised. Most of the burials in York were made in its grounds, the shareholders, after some years of dividends varying between 0 and 6% but averaging just over 3%, were about to see the return on their capital increase considerably and, moreover, the population of the City was still growing rapidly. Although £1,000 was still owed to the bank and other creditors, the provision of the cemetery had been achieved without expense to the ratepayers, costly litigation and high burial charges that were experienced elsewhere. The York Public Cemetery Company 'exempted York from any public burden of this kind', and provided burial for the citizens at a lower rate than most towns with harmony between the different religious denominations who shared a common resting place. The cemetery committee thought that

it must be very satisfactory to the shareholders to witness the success which has attended their efforts to establish a peaceful and beautiful cemetery where the remains of themselves and fellow citizens may repose undisturbed till the morning of resurrection and however much some persons object to this mode of providing burial places yet as after various attempts and many years of delay no other mode could be devised and as pecuniary profit was not the object of the Establishment of this Company, your Committee cannot think there is much force in the objection.[42]

NOTES

1. Mrs Edwin *Gray Papers and Diaries of a York Family* (1927) p 268; Hugh Murray Murray's York Pedigrees MS at York Reference Library.
2. Deed of Settlement of the York Public Cemetery Company (1927).
3. W. & J. Hargrove *The New Guide for Strangers and Residents in the City of York* (1838) p 150.
4. *Yorkshire Gazette* 19 November 1836; 28 January 1837.
5. *Yorkshire Gazette* 8 April 1837.
6. W. & J. Hargrove, op. cit. in note 3, p 150; *Yorkshire Evening Press* 15 January 1885; J.C. Loudon On the Laying out, Planting, and Managing of Cemeteries (1843) p 24.
7. *Yorkshire Gazette* 9 September 1837.
8. *Yorkshire Gazette* 16 September 1837.
9. John Malden, 'The Walker Iron Foundry, York, c1825-1923' *York Historian I* (1976) p 48; W. Thomlinson Walker Pattern Book (no date) MS deposited at Castle Museum, York, PI 24.
10. *Yorkshire Gazette* 20 July 1838; YCA Acc 247/155/1 MS draft for Annual Report 1840.
11. C. Brooks *Mortal Remains* (1989) p 66.
12. *Yorkshire Gazette* 7 October 1837.
13. *Yorkshire Gazette* 16 Sept 1837; *Mechanics' Magazine* Vol xxvii (10 June 1837) pp 145/6.
14. Deed of Settlement of the York Public Cemetery Company (1927) p 15; *Yorkshire Herald* 17 March 1906.
15. *Yorkshire Gazette* 20 July 1838.
16. J.C. Loudon op. cit. in note 6, p 1; W. & J. Hargrove, op. cit. in note 3, p 152; *Yorkshire Gazette* 29 July 1848.
17. *Yorkshire Gazette* 3 August 1878, 28 July 1888.
18. W. & J. Hargrove, op. cit. in note 3, pp 151/2; Elton & Foster *Yorkshire Piety and Persuasion* (1985) p 68; Leeds University, Brotherton Library, MS 421/119/6, 7, 10, 12, 13, 15.
19. A. Armstrong *Stability and Change in an English Country Town* (1974) p 92; YCA Acc 239/22/1, Register of Burials 1.

20. Edwin Chadwick *Supplementary Report on the Results of the Special Inquiry into the Practice of Interment in Towns* (1843).
21. YCA Acc. 247/155 MS drafts for Cemetery Company Annual Reports, 1850 and 1853; *Yorkshire Gazette* 14 August 1847.
22. YCA Ac. 247/155/2 Annual Report 1848.
23. W. & J. Hargrove, op. cit. in note 3, pp 151/2; YCA Ace. 247/155/1 MS draft for Cemetery Company Annual Reports, 1840.
24. *Yorkshire Gazette* 14 August 1847, 29 July 1848; YCA Acc 247/37.
25. *Yorkshire Gazette* 14 August 1847.
26. YCA Acc. 247/155/3b Annual Report 1849; *Yorkshire Gazette* 4 August 1849.
27. YCA Acc. 247/155/4a Annual Report 1851; J.C. Loudon *On the Laying Out, Planting, and Managing of Cemeteries* (1843, reprinted 1981) Introduction by J. S. Curl p 19.
28. A. Armstrong op. cit. in note 18, p 152/3; YCA Acc. 239/22/1.
29. *Yorkshire Gazette* 8 Aug 1846, 14 Aug 1847; YCA Acc. 247/155/2 Annual Report 1848.
30. YCA Acc. 247/155/1 MS Draft Annual Report 1840; YCA Acc. 247/155/2 Annual Report 1848; YCA Acc. 247/155/46 MS Draft Annual Report 1853; YCA Acc 239/22/2, Register of Burials II.
31. YCA Ace. 107/65; *Yorkshire Gazette* 4 May & 27 July 1861.
32. A. E. Hargrove *The Baneful Custom of Interment in Towns and the Present State of York Graveyards* (1847) pp 15, 16, 18-21.
33. *Yorkshire Gazette* 17 July 1847.
34. *Yorkshire Gazette* 4 June 1853, 15 July 1854.
35. *Yorkshire Gazette* 28 October 1854, 11 November 1854, 18 November 1854, 23 December 1854.
36. YCA BB5 pp 381-4.
37. *Yorkshire Gazette* 25 July 1857.
38. *Yorkshire Gazette* 15 Aug 1857.
39. *Yorkshire Gazette* 5 August 1865
40. *York Herald* 9 February 1856; YCA Ace. 247/155/55b, Letter from J.P. Pritchett to Burial Acts Office, 25 February 1858.
41. YCA BB5 pp 89/90, 314; YCA BC16/4 p 72; *Yorkshire Gazette* 26 August 1854.
42. YCA Acc. 247/155/39, MS Draft Annual Report, 1849.

3: *A Fine and Private Place'* – *Consolidation and Prosperity*

'The grave's a fine and private place, But none I think do there embrace.'
Andrew Marvell, To his Coy Mistress

The committee of the York Public Cemetery Company was surprised to receive 47 applicants for the vacancy created by the death of William Powell Ruddock on 26 April 1861, perhaps a testimonial to the success of the enterprise or, possibly, that the salary of £80 a year was particularly attractive. They selected Stephen Ansell of the Industrial School, Leeds, as the new superintendent of the grounds, a decision that had to be confirmed at a special meeting of shareholders, in advance of the annual general meeting to be held on 29 July, in order that he could take up his duties without delay. Ansell moved into the cemetery lodge where a small office (approx. 18ft x 7ft) had been created by enclosing the open portico. This enabled the business of the company to be conducted without interfering with the privacy of the superintendent and his family as well as ensuring the constant supervision of the grounds that was made necessary because of the constant theft of plants from both the graves and the formal flower beds.[1]

Besides the new superintendent the cemetery company was to undergo, during the 1860s, an almost complete change in its management. The next change occurred at the beginning of November 1864 when the Revd Josiah Crofts resigned after 21 years as cemetery chaplain. When he had taken the post in 1843 the burials in the cemetery just exceeded 200 and he had performed the last rites at 109 of them. In his last year five times as many bodies had been brought to the cemetery for burial but his share was only 123. Since June 1852, however, he had been assisted by his curate, the Revd John Edward Mayne Young who conducted his first burial service on 7 June that year, only one day after he had been ordained as a deacon. In Croft's last year as cemetery chaplain Young officiated at 620 interments.

On 30 September 1856 Young had been involved in an incident described by Thomas Snowden as 'one of the most unjustifiable outrages on private feeling and common decency it has ever been my lot to witness.' Snowden had been at the cemetery to attend the funeral of a friend, arranged at first, to take place at 4 pm but delayed, for the convenience of Young, by half an hour. The funeral party did not arrive until 4.50 pm and then was kept waiting for a further 15 minutes while Young conducted another burial service. The cemetery clerk then informed the waiting mourners that the chaplain had to be in York for a 'party' and did not have the time to read the usual service but would, if required, officiate at the graveside. On hearing this the undertaker tried in vain to get Young to perform his customary duties but he would not – 'attired in his robes and with the flush of ill-dissembled anger on his face, he stood immovable'.

The Revd H. Newton of St Cuthbert's sprang to the defence of his colleague who was determined to ignore the accusation. The funeral had been delayed because the chaplain, far from wishing to indulge in pleasures of the flesh, had been attending a clerical conference which did not finish its session until 4 pm and was to resume at 6 pm. Young had designed a graveside burial service for the 'dilatory party' which he, Newton, could attest was, 'in many parts of England all that is required or used and, indeed, deemed quite sufficient'. On hearing this W. Welburn, junior, of Goodramgate, who had no connection with either of the parties involved or the incident itself, took it upon himself, as a churchman, to write to the Archbishop of York for a ruling on the form of service used. The Archbishop considered that the part of the burial service which was usually read in church was a necessary part of the service and not optional on the part of the officiating clergyman. It could only be omitted in the case of death from an infectious disease or when the corpse was in such a state that taking the coffin into a church would be prejudicial to the health of those in attendance. Young and Newton, through the columns of the press, had been firmly put in their place.[2]

Croft was, at the time of his resignation, aged 69 and had not undertaken his duties at the cemetery since March 1864. The increased workload, on top of his parochial duties at St Saviour's, had obviously become too much for him. He died on 25 May 1866 and was buried in the cemetery amongst the remains of so many of his former clients. The cemetery committee sought to find a successor by an advertisement in the local papers asking candidates to apply in writing by 14 November 1864 to the office of the secretaries, Richardson and Gutch, where they could ascertain the duties of the post. The chaplain was now to be paid a salary instead of receiving a fee of 2s 0d for each burial performed. While the fees paid in the previous year had amounted to £97 the average was £88 a year so the salary was fixed at £90 a year (plus laundering of surplices), £10 a year greater than the superintendent, whose salary was not raised to this level until July 1866! At the same time the fee for dissenting ministers was raised from 1s 6d to 2s 0d a service. If the committee had hoped to find a throng of candidates outside the secretary's office at 11 am on 15 November, similar to that applying for the superintendent's post three years earlier, it was disappointed. Only two clerics presented themselves for interview, the Revd J.M. Thompson, curate of St Crux, and the Revd Henry Vaughan Palmer, curate of St Margaret's, Walmgate. It is possible that Palmer was appointed to the chaplaincy because of the proximity of his church to the cemetery which would make him readily available for his duties there. He had become curate of St Margaret's in August 1861, his first appointment in the established church after leaving the Unitarian ministry three years earlier.[3]

The final change in the cemetery hierarchy was made in 1868. When James Pigott Pritchett, architect and a driving force in the management of the cemetery, died on 23 May that year the surviving trustees suddenly realised that their number had been reduced by death from 22 to five, John Robert Mills, who had ceased to be a shareholder, James Chadwick, Thomas Hands, Rev. John Kendrick and George Leeman. This was below the legal minimum specified in the Deed of Settlement and action was urgently required to find some new trustees to whom the estates and premises could be 'with all convenient speed, conveyed, assigned, transferred, and assured respectively'. At the next annual general meeting on 21 July the committee proposed 22 people, including all four of the shareholding survivors, as trustees but when the new trust deed was signed on 12 September four were no longer included.[4] The new trustees were:

Revd Robert William Bilton Hornby
Michael Varvill, Lead Merchant
Richard Audus Clark

William Whytehead, Solicitor
William Gray, Solicitor
William Richardson, Solicitor
John Roper, Brewer
John Harrison Thomas, Solicitor
Thomas Ellis
The Revd John Kendrick
George Leeman, Solicitor
Thomas Hands, Auctioneer
William John Hands, Auctioneer
Joseph Agar, Currier
David Hill, Currier
Michael Charlton
James Meek, Jnr, Glass Manufacturer
Edwin Wade, Surgeon Dentist

One of the four people proposed, but not formalised as trustees, was George Wilson of Nunthorpe Grove, junior partner in Meek, Spence and Wilson, glass manufacturers. He was a shareholder, having bought his three shares in 1862, but had also just agreed to sell the cemetery company, at a good profit to himself, some additional land on either side of the south east corner of the existing ground. When the previous purchase to extend the cemetery had been made in 1848 it had been calculated that the needs of York could be met for the next 100 years but, with the application of the London Burial Board rules in 1856, the effective space in the extension was reduced by nearly 50% and more land was necessary to ensure the future prosperity of the company. In recognition of this a contingency fund was started in 1864 when £100, which would have otherwise been used to increase the 6% dividend which was paid to shareholders that year, was invested in North Eastern Railway debentures.[5]

In 1846 William Plows, stonemason and owner of Belle Vue House, a Strawberry Hill Gothic extravaganza, which he had built adjacent to the Retreat in 1833, bought the two Lamel Hill closes for £1,500. Plows seems to have got into some financial difficulties and was eventually forced to sell his house and land. The purchaser was Charles Etty, brother of the artist, William Etty RA, and a sugar fabricant from Probolingo, Java, who wanted to establish a home for his family in his native city. He changed the name of the house to Java Hall. William Plows had already sold, in 1850, one acre of the Lamel Hill closes to the east of what was

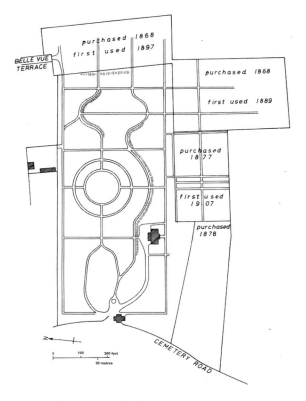

BELLE VUE
TERRACE

purchased 1868
first used 1897

purchased 1868

first used 1889

purchased 1877

first used 1907

purchased 1878

CEMETERY ROAD

z

0   100   200 feet

50 metres

Plan 5 – York Cemetery 1868–1910

to become Belle Vue Terrace to George Hutchinson, a wine and spirit merchant, and, in July 1852, half an acre on the other side to Francis Lyth and John Whitfield for speculative building. Charles Etty paid £2,750, a building land price, for the remaining 5¼ acres on 7 December in the same year. But he did not have long to enjoy his new home, if, indeed, he ever lived there, for he died in Java on 4 December 1856 and his family, who were to take Dutch nationality, decided to sell the York property. In June 1859 their London agents, Finlay, Hodgson & Co., sold what was left of the Lamel Hill closes to George Wilson for £950, an agricultural land price. Thus when the cemetery company decided, in 1868, to extend their land Wilson was able to meet their needs for £1,400 and make a cool profit of £450. He would have been in a more invidious position than he already was as a shareholder if, as a trustee of the cemetery company, he had been seen to use his position for his personal gain.[6]

Although the cemetery company did not buy the additional land until 12 September 1868 it had had it under consideration for some considerable time before. In December 1861, shortly after George Wilson had acquired the Lamel Hill closes, the company sought and obtained from the Home Secretary permission to use the close on the south of the cemetery as a burial ground. On 17 April 1871, three years after gaining possession of all Wilson's land, the remaining part of the land was approved for burial and, after laying the paths, all that remained to be done to make it ready for use was its consecration. Archbishop William Thompson agreed to perform the ceremony on 9 April 1872 and was greeted at the chapel by William Richardson, accompanied by four other members of the cemetery committee, who presented the petition for consecration to the prelate. After it had been read to the assembled witnesses by Henry Hudson, Registrar of the Province and Diocese of York, the Archbishop and a number of clergy, attired in their surplices, walked to the new ground where the 49th psalm was recited and the ceremony was completed by the reading of the deed of consecration by Henry Hudson.[7] These extensions were not, however, to be used for some years – the area to the south (section A) first, in 1893, entirely for private burials, and then the eastern extension of the new ground in 1899 for public burials.

The cemetery now covered 16½ acres and was more than sufficient for immediate requirements so the newly consecrated land was let out as pasture bringing in an income of £16 in 1876.[8] Nevertheless the company realised that its long term existence depended on its having as much land for burial as possible, particularly as the London Burial Board rule had limited the number of the grave spaces in the extensions. It, thus, decided to increase its land whenever an opportunity presented itself. It did not have long to wait for, in 1876, Joseph Agar, a trustee, having achieved such success in the leather business established in York by his grandfather in 1783, had recently taken the final step to complete his gentrification, the moving of his household to a large mansion in the suburbs. This he renamed Kilburn House after the village in the North Riding from which his grandfather had come to take up an apprenticeship to a currier in the City in 1775, and he wished to extend its grounds. Some 6½ acres of land belonging to a Mr Laycock, with a small portion lying on the southern boundary of the cemetery, was auctioned on 30 November 1876 at the Sea Horse Hotel in Fawcett Street and Agar was the successful bidder at £4,400 (£666 an acre). On 27 November he had signed a formal agreement with the cemetery company to sell it the area, measuring 8,469 square yards, adjacent to its land. But this time, to avoid any suspicion of a shareholder profiting from a transaction with his own company, a clause was inserted in the agreement that the price was to be fixed by Edward Taylor, architect, on behalf of Joseph Agar and Charles Hornsey, land surveyor, for the cemetery company. In the event they were unable to agree and another architect, William Atkinson, was appointed as umpire. For a fee of £3 he decided, on 2 June 1877, that the price should be £900, at £514 an acre obviously judged to be of less value than the remainder of the land which Agar added to his estate.[9]

Only one more piece of land lay on the cemetery's southern boundary and this came on the market later the next year. In 1832 William Reaston of Thorganby had acquired 2¼ acres known as Wheat Sheaf Field. He died in 1856 but it was not until 1878 that his executors decided to sell it. It was put up for auction at George Acton's Ebor Sales Room in Low Ousegate on 7 March and the cemetery company committee was the successful bidder at £2,600 but it had to wait until the annual general meeting in August for the shareholder's approval of the purchase. In spite of opposition from Edward Thomas Snowden, who thought it a great extravagance and proposed that it should be resold, wiser counsels prevailed. After hearing from the chairman, Alderman Sir James Meek, that it was probably the only opportunity they would get to buy it and that it made the cemetery complete, enabling the company to supply the wants of the City for a long time to come, the committee's action was agreed and the land was conveyed to the trustees on 22 October. The matter obviously rankled in the minds of some of the shareholders as Sir James Meek had to explain the company's philosophy of land purchase again at the annual general meeting on 6 July 1880. The cemetery now covered nearly 21 acres and although the last two extensions had cost £3,500, an average of £868 an acre, the overall cost was a little less than £280 an acre. This was not correct; the company had in fact expended £7,787 which was £374 an acre! Meek was convinced that it would have been very short-sighted, a cause for lasting regret, if the purchase had not been made. As the site had been wanted for building there would have been no other opportunity. All the land available in the vicinity of the cemetery had now been acquired. [10]

The cemetery company was, by now, in a healthy financial position. Since 1870 it had paid a 10% dividend, occasionally enhanced by a bonus – £2 a share in 1874, which made the dividend an effective 30%, and £1 in 1876, equivalent to 20%.[11] At the same time, since 1864 it had been purchasing railway debentures as a land purchase contingency fund. But in the 10 years since the previous purchase the fund had not accumulated enough to cover the £3,500 expended on the recently acquired land. The authorised share capital of the company was £6,000, divided into 600 shares of £10 each, and after the initial allocation of 328 in 1837 the total sold had crept slowly up to 525 by 1854. It stayed at that figure until 1879 when, to raise the balance of the purchase money, the existing shareholders authorised the sale of the remaining 75 shares at public auction. Previously shares had only been disposed of privately between individuals so this public sale would be the first real test of the shares' market price. In the event £1,509 7s 6d (£20 2s 6d a share) was raised. The shareholders must have been delighted to find that, in addition to receiving a good boost to cemetery funds, their capital had doubled in value. Nevertheless, with some unexpected expenditure on the cemetery boundary walls and fences, the bank loan, after this injection of cash, was still £1,040 16s 4d but it was confidently expected that this could be easily paid out of revenue over the next few years.[12]

Before the city centre graveyards were closed the cemetery hearse was used for just over a third of the funerals (on average 166 a year). This fairly intense use meant that, in addition to the cost of hiring a horse to pull it, constant expenditure was needed to keep it in good repair. Even with these outgoings the hearse hire charge of 3s 0d a funeral was sufficient to allow a small profit to be made. However after thirty years of use the hearse was coming to the end of its life and a new one was bought in 1867 and, at the same time, a new coach house was built. For a short time after this both hearses were in use but, in spite of a doubling in the number of burials in the cemetery, the average use of a hearse fell to 152 occasions a year in the 1870s, now only an eighth of all funerals. In November 1870, to cover rising costs, the hire fees were raised to 4s 6d for people who lived in houses rated at less than £5 a year, 6s 0d between £5 and £10 a year and 7s 6d for all others. After paying for licences for both hearses until 1876 the company decided that this was unnecessary expenditure and retired the older of the two which had had a longer life than its replacement was to have. After only 20 years it too was retired in 1887 when not only was a new hearse bought but a horse as well. The hire fee now had to cover all the costs of stabling, feeding and farriery but it must have been thought that this was cheaper than hiring a horse.[13]

Whether or not reckless driving of the cemetery or undertaker's hearses was responsible, all four of the entrance gates had to be extensively repaired in 1876, followed, in 1880, by their complete replacement in a less ornate form. It does not seem possible that the original gates supplied by the Walker Iron Foundry in 1837 could have worn out in only 43 years as many other contemporary gates supplied by this firm have lasted to the present day. Indeed the 1880 gates are still in service 128 years later and have not yet reached the end of their useful life. The inescapable conclusion is that the 1837 gates were prematurely replaced because of some external but undefined damage. The presence today of a metal bollard at the base of the pillar of the northernmost carriage gate confirms that some protection was needed from vehicles coming from the City, the most regular direction of approach, and cutting the corner as they turned in to the cemetery.[14]

While the number of buildings in the cemetery had been increased in 1867 by a new coach house, there was a possibility, in 1872, that the grounds would be further graced by a mortuary. The Town Clerk had written to the cemetery company on 23 December 1871 asking if it would be prepared to provide a building to which the bodies of persons who had died of contagious or infectious diseases could be removed to from their homes or the workhouse to await burial. On 6 January 1872, after a meeting between the cemetery company, the Board of Health and the York Union of Guardians of the Poor, the Town Clerk was informed that there was no objection to the principle but a plan was required before final approval could be given. The site selected for this building, designed by the City Engineer who estimated it would cost about £200 and to be paid for by the Board of Health and the

Elevations of the mortuary chapel which York Corporation, in 1872, wanted to erect near the Belle Vue Terrace entrance to the cemetery. Because of opposition from the local residents the proposal was dropped.

Guardians, was in the north east corner of the cemetery near the gates into Belle Vue Terrace. When George Hutchinson, the wine and spirit merchant, who had built a large house on his acre of ground on the east side of Belle Vue Terrace, heard of the proposal he announced that he proposed to take legal measures to prevent the erection of the mortuary and the use of Belle Vue Terrace as an approach – 'nimbyism' is not a 20th century phenomenon! While the cemetery company approved the design it informed the Town Clerk on 3 February that it was not prepared to give assent to the mortuary being built unless it was indemnified against any loss or expense in any proceedings brought by Mr Hutchinson or any of his 18 neighbours, who, worried about the effect the mortuary would have on the value of their property, had also sent a round robin to the Corporation. The obvious solution was to resite the building on the opposite side of the cemetery away from any houses but the Council, on hearing on 6 March that the company could not agree to this suggestion, dropped the proposal. The residents of Belle Vue Terrace had won the day![15]

The chapel 'though solidly built and not unattractive in its external appearance' was the subject of many complaints from the people who attended funeral services there. Its want of comfort and lack of heating and ventilation led to it being nicknamed 'The Dutch Barn'. As early as 1872 A NATIVE OF YORK had described it as a '3rd class railway waiting room looking place' whose mean appearance was out of keeping with the well managed grounds. He also drew attention to the apparently unsafe state of the roof and, in addition, complained that mourners experienced inconvenience in having to wait outside while waiting for a funeral 'for want of proper accommodation'. Sir James Meek told the annual general meeting in 1881, and again in 1883, that some of the profits would shortly be needed to refit and improve the interior of the chapel but it was not until 1884 that the need to do something was discussed in detail.[16]

William Whytehead, who had for some time been a protagonist for improvement, said that the bald and dull interior was offensive to some minds. It should be possible, without great expense, to remove the two 'frightful pews' and the heavy benches and replace them with 'such seating as used in most places of worship in the present day'. A little decoration would also make it look lighter and more pleasing to the eye. He proposed that an architect be engaged to reseat and improve the chapel. Alderman Joseph Agar disagreed; he did not think the chapel needed repainting; it was somewhat old fashioned but perfectly comfortable and fencing the grounds was a greater priority. When his amendment was put to the meeting it was narrowly carried. Whytehead then proposed that the committee should employ an architect and, having received his report on the 'best mode of improving the interior of the chapel', should deal with the matter as they saw fit. Alderman Agar again opposed this new proposal as such an important decision should be made by the shareholders and not the committee. He thought that the only way to improve the place at all was to pull the whole of it down! His motive, as it would appear more openly at the next annual general meeting, was to ensure that the maximum dividend was paid to the shareholders. This second proposal by Whytehead now received unanimous support although a number of shareholders abstained.[17]

With this mandate the committee lost no time in making the improvements to the chapel that the citizens of York, if not all the shareholders of the cemetery company, required. Edward Taylor, a local architect of Stonegate, was asked to make suggestions for remodelling the interior with 'more modern notions' of comfort and ecclesiastical appearance. The alterations, which he recommended, were completed by January 1885. The high backed pews were replaced by open pitch pine stalls with carved ends and an arcaded front rail with round topped arches supported on Tuscan columns, simple reading desks were substituted for the stilted box pulpits, the aisles were laid with oak parquet flooring and the catafalque, with its now

The interior of the chapel, seen here in 1944, with the pews and catafalques installed in 1884 to improve its appearance and comfort.
[Photograph - G. B. Wood]

redundant mechanism for lowering coffins into the catacombs below (no more interments were made in the catacombs after August 1881), was removed and

The 1884 alterations also included a small vestry for the cemetery chaplain, constructed over the rear entrance to the catacombs. It was entered by a doorway knocked through the wall under the centre window.

[Photograph - Helen Kirk 1982]

replaced with a number of coffin turntables. The chapel was now thoroughly warmed by two Musgrave's stoves, one at each end with chimney pipes let into the walls, and ventilation was provided by circular cast iron grills in the ceiling. Having looked after the comforts of the congregation Taylor also provided for the needs of the officiating clergymen, particularly the cemetery chaplain, who was now conducting several funerals every day and had no privacy between services. A doorway was made in the centre of the back wall of the chapel and a small vestry was built on supporting walls over the entrance to the catacombs. The alterations were carried out by G. Simpson & Son of Heworth while J. Thomas of York was responsible for the painting and decorating of the walls and ceiling which afterwards presented `a cheerful and pleasant appearance whilst quiet and harmonious in tone and colour'.[18]

Another problem which was to beset the cemetery company over a number of years was Sunday burials. While the arrangements for an interment could only be made with the cemetery superintendent on weekdays, including Saturday, at least one day before the funeral, burials could take place on Sundays between the hours of public worship.[19] This was of particular benefit to the poor who, working long hours on six days a week, were unable to take time off to bury their relatives without losing at least half a day's pay. That the working class took advantage of this concession can be seen from the fact that, during the first three decades after the opening of the cemetery (1837-1866), Sunday, with 21% of all interments, was the most popular day exceeding the next most popular day, Wednesday, by a quarter. With only one day available to them the working class had to keep the bodies of their dead relatives in their homes, certainly until the Sunday after the death or even the Sunday following, possibly for nine or ten days. Dr Holland of the Burial Acts Office wrote to James Piggott Pritchett in 1858 to suggest that much might be done to prevent bodies being brought to the cemetery in an offensive state if the cemetery company would abolish its practice of allowing Sunday funerals.[20]

Figure i   *Burials by Day of Week*

	1837-46	1847-56	1857-66	1867-76	1877-86	1887-96	1897-1906
Mon	238	733	1151	1666	2004	2211	2224
Tue	274	995	1740	1864	2300	2270	2164
Wed	327	974	1713	1944	2258	2358	2363
Thu	289	862	1504	1602	1934	1878	2035
Fri	285	901	1449	1518	1722	1654	1599
Sat	132	517	902	1492	2353	2573	2667
Sun	402	1320	2247	1353	528	112	131
Total	1947	6302	10706	11439	13139	13056	12980

But it was not the offensive state of some bodies brought to the cemetery for burial but vandalism and theft that moved Sir James Meek to raise the question of interment on Sundays at the 1869 annual general meeting. Visitors to the cemetery on Sundays had been abusing the privilege by doing mischief and desecrating the company's property, a practice 'painful to all possessed of proper feelings'. Flowers, planted on graves, were pilfered by passers-by, including those 'whose sex and position in life might have been thought a guarantee against an unfeeling act'. The company did not wish to close the cemetery entirely on Sundays but, in an attempt to solve these problems, it decided that all interments on that day should be made before 10am. Admission, therefore, would not be permitted after 9.30 am which would allow mourners and officiating ministers the opportunity of attending their places of worship. The new times were to start on 1 September despite a plea from E.T. Snowden that they would make difficulties for the poor who could only bring their dead for burial on Sundays. Henry Joseph Dennett, who had visited the cemetery on Sundays for many years, thought the reasons given for the closure a libel as he had never seen the graves desecrated or anything objectionable done. He had intended to attend the meeting, although not a shareholder, to present a petition, signed by 743 persons, against the proposal (he had had only four refusals to sign) but, having been misinformed about the date, continued his canvass until he had 1650 signatures, a sufficient expression of the public opinion against a measure which would entail upon the working man an additional expense of at least £1. To protect the flowers 'W', in writing to the press, proposed that numerous notices should be displayed, as in Scarborough cemetery, warning that offenders would be punished.[21] The immediate effect of these restricted hours was that in the next decade (1867-76) the number of Sunday burials fell to 12% and faded away to negligible proportion by 1880 while the cemetery business remained sensibly constant until the First World War. The result was that the working class then made Saturday its chosen day for funerals. This coincided with the advent of the half holiday on that day for some workers, a practice which had become more general by the 1890s.

The chapel can be seen through the trunks of the lime trees which line the path dividing the original area of the cemetery from later extensions to the south.

[Photograph - Helen Kirk 1982]

The closure of the cemetery on Sundays also meant that many people lost the only opportunity they had of visiting the graves of their deceased relatives or friends. At the annual general meeting in 1885 a Mr Marchant spoke on their behalf and suggested opening the cemetery for a limited period. He was informed that, contrary to his understanding, the cemetery was open to the friends of those buried there. It was the general public who were excluded as it was thought that the friends might be 'disturbed rather than benefited' during their visits if the distinction was not made. The superintendent would be unable to keep a proper check on people if admissions were indiscriminate, 'immoralities would be perpetrated in the sacred enclosure' and idlers would be tempted to make use of it. Pressure was brought to bear on the cemetery authorities by numerous letters in the columns of the newspapers with the result that they eventually relented and in 1887 opened the cemetery to all on Sunday afternoons between 2 and 4pm. A great number of orderly people took advantage of this concession but PATERFAMILIAS would have preferred closing time extended to 5pm, as it was in all other large towns, even if the company had to put an attendant on the gate to exclude dogs and unaccompanied children. The cemetery company paid large dividends and it seemed unreasonable to him to limit those who had paid heavily for their little plots to just two hours on the most convenient day of the week. The stereotyped objection of the company that the nearness of the cemetery to the barracks made it undesirable to open it on Sundays was an unwarrantable reflection on 'the brave fellows who wear the Queen's uniform' as, on Sunday morning, they were in barracks or attending church parades.[22]

The Revd Henry Vaughan Palmer, the cemetery chaplain, died on 29 July 1877 and by 6 August the duties had been taken over by the Revd George Henry Hewison, who had been second master at Archbishop Holgate's Grammar School from 1863 until he resigned to become rector of St Dennis, Walmgate, in 1873. Palmer had been receiving a salary of £100 a year when he died and Hewison, on appointment, was given the same. In 1888 he applied to the cemetery committee for an increase to £120 a year. The committee decided that they could not agree to this but had to get its decision confirmed at the annual general meeting on 19 July. It would have been no surprise to them when the shareholders, who had just voted themselves a dividend of 10% plus a bonus of 10s 0d a share (equivalent to a 15% dividend), agreed with it. Hewison, not apparently discouraged by this, kept the post until his retirement on 3 April 1902 even though he had moved from St Dennis to Moor Monkton in 1901, two years after he had added the chaplaincy of the York Union Workhouse to his workload. He died on 29 January

The Revd George Henry Hewison, cemetery chaplain 1877 – 1903, who performed 18542 funeral services during this period.

1903 and was replaced on 6 May by the Revd Archibald Bailey Armstrong, rector of St Margaret's, Walmgate, at the same salary of £100 a year.[23] During his time as cemetery chaplain Hewison officiated at 18,542 funerals, 55.5% of all burials during that period, and an average of 713 a year!

In 1872 Stephen Ansell resigned as gardener and superintendent in spite of having had his salary increased from £90 to £100 a year less than two years previously. The committee must have been gratified to find that the number of applicants for the vacancy exceeded the 47 it had had when Ruddock died in 1861. From 66 candidates on this occasion it selected Thomas Brown of Boston, at a salary of £100 a year, and got a superintendent who not only showed great loyalty to the cemetery company, serving it for 37 years until shortly before his death at the age of 82 on 24 December 1909, but who was also to build up the role of the stone-yard until it provided the major contribution to the revenues of the enterprise. When Brown was appointed all the small profit that the stone-yard made came from providing new monuments for the cemetery and making alterations to existing ones. But all that was to change; by inserting advertisements in the local newspapers and street directories Brown increased the profits in this department over four-fold by supplying stone-work for other graveyards as well as the cemetery itself. His efforts were well recognised by grateful shareholders, who were now receiving regular bonuses on top of a basic 10% dividend. In 1883 Brown's salary was increased from £110 to £130 a year followed two years later by a further increase of £20 a year. The same increase was proposed in 1887, a year in which no bonus was paid to the shareholders, but they resolved to give him just £10 a year instead, the last increase he was to receive. His salary was to remain at £160 a year until he retired when he was rewarded with a small pension of £6 13s 4d a month.[24] The other outcome of his success was that the small office, constructed within the portico of the lodge and now too small for the extra staff needed to deal with the increased business, was pulled down in 1892 and replaced with a larger one extending forward to the carriage gate-post, leaving only one gate for pedestrians.[25]

In an attempt to recover part of the loss on interments the company revised some of its charges in November 1870. The 'at-cost' price of 4s 6d for burying people in public graves who lived in houses with a rateable value under £5 a year was retained but two new categories were introduced – 6s 6d for occupants of houses with a rateable value under £10 a year and 10s 6d for all other persons. Except for brick

YORK CEMETERY COMPANY

EVERY DESCRIPTION OF

Monumental Work

IN

GRANITE, MARBLE AND STONE

EXECUTED BY EXPERIENCED WORKMEN.

INSCRIPTIONS Neatly and Care-fully inscribed; Imperishable letters in Marble, etc. ESTIMATES GIVEN.

Thomas Brown, Manager.

The appointment of Thomas Brown as cemetery superintendent brought a change in the fortunes of the stone yard. He advertised its services far and wide and increased its work four fold. These advertisements appeared in York street directories between 1885 and 1902.

vaults, raised by £1 10s 0d to £11 10s 0d, only the charges for public burials, by far the largest category, were altered. The immediate result was that the small loss on interments in 1870 was turned into an equally small profit in 1871 but in five years the loss had increased considerably. Further fairly drastic measures were taken in 1894 when it was decided to make an additional charge for Sunday interments – 4s 6d in all the three classes of public burial and 10s 0d for burial in

Figure ii

	Profits of Stone yard			Profits on Interments and Grave Sales			Number of burials
	£	s	d	£	s	d	
1870	119	0	1	577	15	11[a]	1197
1871	100	8	7	536	13	4[b]	1152
1876	314	15	11	515	2	0[c]	1244
1877	327	14	11	387	13	0[d]	1212
1884	500	6	6	486	16	4	1247
1893	541	19	6	387	1	2	1289

a includes loss of 9s 1d on interments
b includes profit of £5 8s 4d on interments
c includes loss of £117 18s 0d on interments
d includes loss off £146 7s 0d on interments

private and second class graves. These increased charges would have considerably affected the poor but may have now encouraged them to bring their bodies for burial on weekdays as the Burial Acts Office had required in 1858.[26]

Even though the cemetery had had a monopoly of burial in York since the beginning of 1855 only three staff were employed in the stone-yard in 1856, two adults at £1 4s 0d a week and one apprentice, William Harbert, who was indentured to Ruddock, the superintendent, for six years in August 1854 at 3s 0d a week. At this time there were three sextons (gravediggers) who were paid 17s 0d a week. In 1878, six years after Brown became superintendent, there were three stonemasons, two earning £1 10s 4d a week, and eight sextons with a basic weekly wage of £1 1s 0d. Thereafter Brown's success in building up the work of the stone-yard was reflected in a steady increase in the number of staff employed there, reaching a maximum of seven in 1892, the year after the cemetery company had, at 1,417, made its then greatest number of burials in one year, a figure only to be exceeded on one occasion, in 1900, when there were 1,518 burials. At the same time the number of sextons had risen to ten and their wages to £1 2s 0d a week. If any of these staff were not at work for any reason they had to sacrifice payment for the time lost. An attempt was made at the annual general meeting in 1885 to allow them a half-day holiday every year without deduction of pay. A more enlightened shareholder suggested that two days paid holiday would be more appropriate! The meeting, however, decided to leave the matter to the committee but the outcome, alas, is not recorded.[27]

A problem that had to be overcome in 1890 was that there were no more spaces for public graves in the original 8¼ acres, the only area not covered by the London Burial Board rules, and an undertaking had been given that, except for family burials, no more than one body would be put in each grave in the newer areas. How the rules were overturned is not known, perhaps they were just ignored, but on 22 May 1890 a new grave was opened at the south end of the new ground bought from Samuel Tuke in an area to be specifically reserved for public burials. With the larger grave size specified by the London Burial Board rules there was now no need to intersperse the public graves among the private ones to give the latter the appearance of more space. In the next 20 years some 4,600 bodies were buried in an area measuring 136ft by 117ft. The number of bodies in each grave varies considerably but the maximum is 48, buried over a period of 25 days. At the rear of this area is a line of unmarked graves, known at the time as 'Flu Walk', where many of the 226 victims of an influenza epidemic that lasted from April to June 1891 were buried. Because of the extra work this produced for the chaplain, the superintendent and his daughter, the shareholders agreed to pay them gratuities totalling £25.[28] A number of the second class graves in the original part of the cemetery that had not been completely filled were, at this time, sold to relatives of one of the occupants who, in consideration of a cheaper price, did not mind having a few strangers at the bottom of their now private family grave!

The cemetery had been valued for rates by Thomas F Hedley of Sunderland on 20 Sept 1867 at a time when the company owned just over 11 acres, the profits were still small and the dividend to shareholders was only 8%. He arrived at a figure of £211 (figure ii) which meant that the company had to pay rates of £47 9s 6d in 1870 (at a poundage of 4s 6d), nearly twice what they had paid in 1848. As the company made more profit so the rateable value rose but the extra land it acquired was, until it was used for its intended purpose, assessed at virtually the rent earned from pasture. In 1899, after an appeal to the Assessment Committee of the York Poor Law Union, the rateable value of the cemetery was reduced to £450 gross and the pasture land, leased out at £47 15s 4d, to £50. Although not satisfied with the former figure the company made no further appeal but in 1900 it was decreased to £424 gross (£364 net) and remained at this level for the next two years despite a considerable fall off in the interment account. The cemetery company, which thought it had paid too much for years, having asked the Assessment Committee, without success, for a reduction, appeared at the Quarter Sessions before the Recorder in January 1905. Its counsel, R.H. Vernon

Figure iii   *Calculation of Rateable Value -1867*

	£	s	d	£	s	d
Receipts - Interments				547	7	5
Stonework				571	9	0
				1118	16	5
Expenditure - Salaries, Wages	546	18	3			
Materials	296	12	2	843	10	5
Net Profit				275	6	0
Tenants Profits				41	0	0
Gross Estimated Rental				234	6	0
Deduct Repairs				23	6	0
Estimated Value (Net)				211	0	0

Wragge, contended, ingeniously, that the stone-yard should be assessed separately from the cemetery which, as a public benefit, entitled it to special consideration. The Recorder, in dismissing the appeal, agreed with Harold Thomas, representing the Overseers, that the assessment was fair. The stone-yard and the cemetery had been rated together since the company was formed and by dutifully paying its rates without comment for so many years it had accepted the method of rating the whole business.[29]

In 1870, when the dividend paid to shareholders first reached 10%, the chairman, Sir James Meek, a second generation trustee, made a statement at the annual general meeting seemingly designed to dispel any criticism that might be made when the public heard of it. 'The object of the company was not to make money but as the cemetery answered and a profit was derived it was only fair and reasonable that the shareholders should receive a suitable dividend for the capital they had embarked, especially as it was known that for very many years no dividend whatever was paid (Hear, Hear).' The second part of his statement, to be repeated on other occasions, was not entirely true. A dividend had been paid in the first three years after the cemetery opened and in the first ten years it had averaged 3¼%. A dividend would have been paid every year after 1846 but in 1849, when the balance in the current account was sufficient to pay 3%, the shareholders decided to forgo a dividend in order to liquidate the debt incurred by purchasing additional land. This was entirely consistent with the principles of the first generation trustees who had been much more concerned with the provision of a decent burial place for their fellow citizens than the prospect of making money out of death.

A year later Sir James said that the affairs of the company were economically managed and no money (that would otherwise reduce the dividend?) was wasted. The cemetery had promoted harmony between all the different religious denominations who used a common resting place, far different from the unseemly strife seen at some cemeteries. In 1878 he commented about the very proper feeling that was abroad against the undue expenditure on funerals. The company's charges had been criticised but he was quite sure that, if any of the parties concerned were to examine the workings of the company, they would find they had no fair cause of complaint. Poor burials were a loss to the company which had absorbed rising wage costs without an increase in its charges. It was very gratifying, said Sir James in 1880, to find, although not to the pecuniary advantage of shareholders, that the health of the locality had improved to such an extent that there had been only 1,199 interments in the year against 1,442 in the previous year. Sir James Meek was not present at the annual general meeting in 1889 but it was left to a Mr Marchant to present the usual *apologia*. He thought of the cemetery as leasehold property and each year it was decreasing in value, effectively depreciating the shareholder's capital. They 'had all the risk and now they ought to have the benefit'. The consciences of the trustees and shareholders were obviously troubled! On the credit side the Inspector of Cemeteries had made a visit to the cemetery in 1889 and had said that if every cemetery was as well conducted there would be no need for any talk about changes.[30]

But in the last quarter of the 19th century profit had became more important than altruism and was achieved, it would appear, by economising in the maintenance of the ground. A NATIVE OF YORK was perturbed to find in July 1876 that, apart from the entrance, the cemetery grounds were in a discreditable state. The public and private graves were covered with coarse grasses and weeds in endless variety, in many places knee deep. An unskilful attempt to chop down some of the 'rubbish' had made appearances worse than before. The cemetery looked painfully desolate and altogether disregarded by the company, a contrast to the 'well managed grounds' of 1872. He was surprised that the company had achieved such a pecuniary good result, a 10% dividend and a bonus, money which, he thought, would have served to keep the grounds in better order. In 1886 additional bonuses, paid in only two previous years, became a regular feature, with the

P.C. John Henry Burdett broke his back fighting a fire at the railway station on 5 February 1905. He died of his injuries on 31 October and was given a civic funeral. His coffin, carried on a Shand Mason fire engine, has just passed the prison walls in Tower Street.

exception of 1887. The consciences of the trustees and shareholders were always salved in the same way; they were merely recouping their capital. Although the balance at the bank in 1887 would have allowed the payment of a 10s 0d bonus the committee decided not to recommend it; the walks needed to be regravelled, a new hearse had to be bought and some of the new land had to be prepared for burial. Joseph Agar took exception to this and moved an amendment that the 10s 0d bonus be paid. When the vote was taken he found that half of the shareholders at the meeting agreed with him. The chairman then had to use his casting vote to ensure that the committee's recommendation was accepted.[31]

The cemetery, however, was a wasting asset. As graves were closed they could not ever, in accordance with the stated objectives of the company, be reopened. In recognition of this the committee decided, in 1849, that every year 3s 4d, the actual cost of the 2½ square yards of land each grave occupied plus a proportion for conveyancing, levelling, planting and laying out paths, should be deducted from the receipts of every one sold. The whole value of the property was diminished by that amount and it would be used to liquidate the company's debts. It was thus necessary to deduct £134 3s 0d from the stock account to cover the 805 grave sites sold since 1837. The same thought was advocated in 1887 by James

Melrose who proposed starting a reserve fund to meet the decreasing value of the cemetery. Edwin Wade, chairman at the 1890 annual general meeting, stressed the point that the company made its profit, not out of interments but the sale of monumental stone-work and the sale of private graves and it must be remembered that the latter was obtained by disposal of its freehold. The shareholders could be in no doubt that the time would come, sooner or later, when the cemetery was full and their income would cease.[32]

In the last decade of the 19th century the shareholders of the York Public Cemetery Company prospered; with the number of burials averaging 1,340 a year, they received an income from their shares of at least 15% and the market price of a £10 share, which reached a peak of £25 in 1892, never fell below £22. Out of nearly 21 acres of land owned by the company only 13 acres was being used for burials and the remainder, let out as pasture, would, it was thought, provide ample space for 100 to 150 years to come. Apart from the Quaker Burial Ground in the grounds of the Retreat in Heslington Road it had no real competitors and a virtual monopoly of burial in York. Although the committee occasionally reminded the shareholders of the eventual demise of the company, this event was sufficiently far in the future to be pushed to the backs of their minds. The possibility of new burial grounds opening near the City, the provision of an alternative means of the disposal of the dead or even the falling death rate, did not unduly disturb their contentment. Thomas Brown, who died at the end of 1909, had seen the fortunes of the cemetery rise to their peak but his successor as superintendent was to see the beginning of the end.

NOTES

1. *Yorkshire Gazette* 27 July 1861.
2. *York Herald* 11, 18, 25 October, 1 November 1856.
3. *Yorkshire Gazette* 2 October 1858, 31 August 1861, 5 November 1864, 28 July 1866; *Yorkshire Herald* 19 November 1864.
4. Deed of Settlement of the York Public Cemetery Company (1927), p18; *Yorkshire Gazette* 25 July 1868.
5. *Yorkshire Gazette* 30 July 1864.
6. *Yorkshire Gazette* 25 July 1868; YCA Acc. 107/52, 66, 70, 70a.
7. *Yorkshire Gazette* 13 April 1872.
8. YCA Acc. 247/155/ Annual Report 1876.
9. YCA Acc. 247/155/76b, f & g.
10. YCA Acc. 247/155/77- *Yorkshire Gazette* 3 August 1878, 10 July 1880.
11. *Yorkshire Gazette* 8 August 1874, 15 July 1876.

12. *Yorkshire Gazette* 2 August 1879, 10 July 1880.
13. *Yorkshire Gazette* 3 August 1867, 28 July 1888; YCA Acc. 247/26.
14. YCA Acc. 247/155/7; *Yorkshire Gazette* 10 July 1880.
15. YCA BC16/5 pp 384, 393/4, 402, 410-12.
16. *York Herald* 13 January 1872; *Yorkshire Gazette* 9 July 1881, 28 July 1883.
17. *Yorkshire Gazette* 19 July 1884, 18 July 1885.
18. *Yorkshire Evening Press* 15 January 1885.
19. W & J. Hargrove *The New Guide for Strangers and Residents in the City of York* (1838) p 152.
20. YCA Ace. 247/55.
21. *Yorkshire Gazette* 24 July 1869; *York Herald* 6 February, 31 July 1869.
22. *Yorkshire Gazette* 18 July 1885; *York Herald* 28 March 1887.
23. *Yorkshire Gazette* 4 August 1877, 28 July 1888, 31 January 1903.
24. YCA Ace. 247/155/6, 7 & 247/76; *Yorkshire Gazette* 22 July 1871, 27 July 1872, 28 July 1883, 19 July 1884, 18 July 1885, 16 July 1887, 15 July 1893, 1 January 1910.
25. York Council Minutes (YCM), p 331.
26. *Charges and Regulations at the York Public Cemetery*, November 1870: Minutes of Committee of York Public Cemetery Company, 21 March 1894.
27. YCA Acc. 107/44; *Yorkshire Gazette*, 18 July 1885.
28. *Yorkshire Gazette* 25 July 1891; York City Council *Report on Influenza and the Influenza Epidemic* of 1918 13 February 1918 p 6.
29. YCA Ace. 247/67; *Yorkshire Gazette* 14 Jan 1905.
30. *Yorkshire Gazette* 4 August 1849, 23 July 1870, 22 July 1871, 3 August 1878, 10 July 1880, 19 July 1889.
31. *Yorkshire Gazette* 22 July 1876, 16 July 1887.
32. YCA Ace. 247/155/3b; *Yorkshire Gazette* 16 July 1887, 18 July 1890.

4: 'God's-Acre'- A Municipal Cemetery?

I like that ancient Saxon phrase, which calls the burial ground God's-Acre

H.W Longfellow God's-Acre

Even before York cemetery had opened, criticisms had been voiced that it was situated inconveniently for the people living on the opposite side of the City, a difficulty that the Archdeacon of York had hoped to overcome by providing four cemeteries, one just outside of each of the principal Bars. In an attempt to allay these criticisms York Public Cemetery Company had published a list of distances of its cemetery from various landmarks in the City which, in its eyes, showed that it was situated as conveniently as one could expect for a cemetery outside the walls. Micklegate Bar was the farthest point listed, 1 mile 140 yards from the cemetery, and the residents of the suburbs that were beginning to grow outside the walls in this area, mostly railway workers and their families, would have to pay to carry their dead for even greater distances, an expense that many could ill afford. It was for this reason that the cemetery company had provided a combined hearse and mourning coach which the poor could hire for only 3s 0d, but even this facility was beyond the means of some people. Although the Corporation had made enquiries early in 1855 and, as a result, decided that the cemetery company could meet all the burial needs of the City, A CITIZEN was moved to write to the *York Herald* in 1856 to ask `when are the Corporation of this City going to bestir themselves to establish another cemetery'. He thought this was necessary to meet the `increasing wants of our increasing population' as well as alleviating the hardship of the poor who lived at the other end of the City. In his opinion the selfishness of a few shareholders who were councillors should not be allowed to stand as an obstacle to an urgent requirement, which 'if not attended to in time, will have to be hastily and rashly determined upon'.[1]

There the matter of another cemetery for York rested for another 22 years until Robert Marchant, a Guardian of the Poor and chairman of the York City and County Funeral and Mourning Reform Association, wrote to the Corporation in 1878 asking if it would not be possible for it to establish its own cemetery which would 'inter at reasonable charges' as well as meeting the needs of the inhabitants of York on the western side of the City. Vested interests were obviously still prominent as the Urban Sanitary Committee, which had five cemetery shareholders among its 14 members, after discussing this letter, minuted that it was `not at present expedient to adopt this proposal'.[2] The problem had been swept under the carpet once again, this time until 1894 when James Morrison Gardiner, a draper of Low Ousegate and John Attlay Shaftoe, a solicitor, both councillors for Castlegate Ward, perhaps remembering the painful scenes in Castlegate on the days of the fortnightly fair, before Skeldergate Bridge and Clifford Street were built, when funeral corteges struggled to get through the press of people assembled there,[3] gave notice that they both intended to propose at the Council meeting on 5 February motions that the Corporation should provide a municipal cemetery. Councillor Gardiner's motion called on the Streets and Building Committee to consider the subject while Councillor Shaftoe's named the Finance and General Purpose Committee. However when the Council finally discussed the matter on 5 March the matter was referred to the Sanitary Committee with the instruction that, in addition, it was to consider any other legal method of disposing of the dead, a recognition that cremation was already gaining acceptance as an alternative at this time.[4]

Although the Town Clerk had been directed on 21 March 1894 to obtain information from the York Cemetery Company and towns and cities with municipal cemeteries the Sanitary Committee was in no hurry to start its deliberations. It was not until 6 October 1897, after Sir Joseph Terry had been asked at a Council meeting on 6 September if his Committee had complied with the Council's instruction, that the Town Clerk was told to tabulate the replies he had received to his earlier enquiries but even then the matter was allowed to lapse for another two years. On 8 February 1900 the Health Committee, which had by then replaced the Sanitary Committee, appointed a special sub-committee to consider the provision of a municipal cemetery with the instruction that it was to report in a month's time. 16 months later the report had still not been produced and a further deadline was set for July 1901 with the usual result – nothing. Then, out of the blue, a letter was received in September from James Backhouse and Son, Nurserymen, offering to sell the Council 20 acres of their land at Holgate for a municipal cemetery. This was the last straw for the sub-committee. Having discussed the Backhouse offer it recommended in October that, as the work of the Health Committee was so great, it should be relieved of this responsibility and replaced by a special Cemetery Committee. [5]

The appointment of the Special Committee seemed, at first, to bring a great improvement in the prospects for a municipal cemetery. By March 1902 it had three sites to consider. In addition to the Backhouse land two plots in Poppleton Road were available. One, belonging to Charles Hornsey, an architect who lived at Ash Villa in Holgate Road, was offered in December 1901 followed in March 1902 by the second, the property of the Revd R.J.P. Tennant, vicar of Acomb. All three owners were then asked for a plan of the area they were willing to sell and the price they wanted for their land but the Committee waited until November before asking the city engineer to mark them on an ordnance plan. The delay was not caused by a waning of the first enthusiasm of the new committee, all busy members of other committees, but by having to wait for the replies from 30 municipalities which had cemeteries under their control. In spite of learning that nearly all of them had to be supported from the rates, the committee, in reporting to the Council on 7 December 1903, was of the opinion that a new cemetery, under Corporation control, was desirable on the south side of the City where there was a large and still increasing population of over 27,000 living at a considerable distance from Cemetery Road. Capital expenditure of about £18,000 would be required and the interest payments on this, together with the cost of management and maintenance, would require an additional rate levy of 1d in the pound.

The report fell short of making a firm recommendation and the Council was asked to decide whether or not a cemetery should be provided and the Committee 'awaited such further instructions (if any) as the Council may be pleased to give'. Faced with this less than enthusiastic support for a municipal cemetery the Council, somewhat enigmatically, merely adopted the report. The committee, chastened by the Council's response, did not reconsider the report until 1 December the next year. It decided to resubmit its previous report without alteration but to be more specific in the recommendation. A resolution was thus added to the report suggesting that the Committee should be instructed to find a suitable site for the cemetery and obtain estimates of the cost of providing and managing it. At its meeting on 2 January 1905 the Council rejected this proposal by 14 votes to 16 with two abstentions – for the first time making a positive decision but one that was to delay consideration of this vexed question for another three years.[6]

A propaganda postcard issued in 1907 in support of the Progressive Party's proposals for the municipalisation of public utilities which, as well as the cemetery, included the waterworks and the tramway system, and plans for a covered market, open moats and a survey of the River Ouse.

At the beginning of the 20th century the Conservatives were in the majority on York Council but the Liberals, with a strong element of the Rowntree family and their employees amongst them, were beginning to make their presence felt in local politics. In 1905 they formed the Progressive Party with a policy of municipalisation of public utilities.[7] A pamphlet, *Towards a Municipal Policy for York*, collecting together articles which had been printed earlier in the *Yorkshire Gazette*, was published in October in the same year which contained the new party's ideas on gas and water supplies, markets, electricity and tramways, slum clearance and education. No mention was made in this pamphlet of a municipal cemetery but Samuel Henry Davies, a Progressive Councillor elected in 1906, a Quaker and the chemist at Rowntree and Co., moved at a Council meeting on 6 April 1908 that a Special Committee should be appointed to consider the provision of such a facility for the City. His motion was defeated on this occasion but when he raised it again on 6 September 1909 he was successful and it was agreed that the Committee would be appointed on 9 November at the start of the next municipal year.[8]

The Progressives were in the minority on this Committee with only five out of its twelve members but Davies was appointed vice-chairman. Nevertheless it set about its task with more energy than any previous Council cemetery committee. At its first meeting on 2 December the information previously obtained from other towns was reviewed, resulting in the Town Clerk being asked to make further enquiries including getting details of the area of land that York Public Cemetery Company still had for burial. On 17 March 1910 the Committee heard that 7¾ acres of York cemetery were unused, adequate for at least another 40 years, with 15 acres adjacent available for expansion but, not deterred by the knowledge that the private cemetery would be a competitor of a municipal cemetery for many years to come, a sub-committee was appointed to visit cemeteries at Middlesborough and Hull which were run by the local authorities. Third class rail fares and out of pocket expenses were allowed for these visits. The findings were obviously favourable as Alderman Thomas Carter, the chairman, and Davies were given the task on 8 September of looking for a suitable site for a municipal cemetery for York.[9]

At the next meeting of the Cemetery Committee on 6 October 1911, with Davies in the chair and the Progressives in the majority, a report was prepared for presentation to the full Council on 9 November. Hull, with a population of 275,000 and a rateable value of £1,182,000, had three cemeteries totalling 120 acres whose expenditure in 1909 had exceeded income by £1,800 which was made good by a rate of ⅓d in the pound. Middlesborough, with a population of 180,000 and a rateable value of £438,500 needed a rate of 1d in the pound to cover the deficit of £1,850 for its one cemetery of 76 acres. The scale of charges in these places and in York was not easy to compare (figure i) but at first sight it appeared that the residents there had the advantage of cheaper burials than the citizens of York. This, and the fact that all other towns and cities in the north of England of the size of York had cemeteries provided by the community, was sufficient to persuade the Committee that the Council should be recommended to purchase 22 acres of land in Poppleton Road which, with the reserves owned by York Public Cemetery Company, would be sufficient for a population of 88,000 for the next 40 years. These figures, which were in conflict with the information supplied by the cemetery company earlier in the year, were based on the Local Government Board's estimate that ¼ acre was needed to serve 1,000 inhabitants for 30 years. It was thought that the annual expenditure would be £1,148, exceeding the income by £703 and requiring a rate of ½d in the pound.[10]

Figure i	York Public Cemetery Company			
	Old Cemetery (private) (Plot size 7ft 6ins x 3ft)	New Cemetery (private) (Plot size 9ft x 4ft)	2nd Class Graves	Public Graves
Purchase Price in Perpetuity	£4 15s, £3 15s, £2 15s	£7 7s, £6 6s, £5 5s, £4 4s		
Total including Interment Fee	£5 15s, £4 15s, £3 15s	£8 7s, £7 6s, £6 5s, £5 4s	£1 15s	6s 6d to10s 6d

Hull Municipal Cemeteries

	Private Graves			
Purchase Price in Perpetuity	£5 5s, £4 4s, £1 7s,	19s 0d		
Total including Interment Fee	£6 6s, £4 19s, £2 2s, £1 11s 6d		£1 1s*	9s 6d
	Burials in 1909: Private - 2273 Public - 828		* space reserved for 14 years	

Middlesbrough Municipal Cemetery

Private Graves only (no public graves)

Purchase Price in Perpetuity	£5 10s, £3 3s, £1 1s	Purchase Price Burial Rights only.	£1 12s, £1 2s, 12s 0d	

The rest of the aldermen and councillors took a different view at the Council meeting on 14 November when the matter was somewhat confused by party political point scoring. Davies proposed the acceptance of the report and was supported by Gascoigne Hastings Fowler Jones who thought that it was very 'necessary that proper oversight and control should be exercised over the disposal of human bodies' and this could be best carried out by the municipal authority! More telling, however, was the fact that the existing cemetery had been, when it opened, on the outskirts of the City but it was now becoming surrounded by houses. The time had arrived, he thought, when the burial of the dead should be removed from the `centre' of the City. Arthur Brown wanted to reject the report because the new cemetery would not pay and the proposed site was not suitable.

What was wanted was 'something more in the nature of a mountain than a field'. Only 17 out of 396 municipal cemeteries paid and because other municipalities had gone mad there was no reason for York to follow suit. Although it was often alleged that the cemetery company was making blood money and paying exorbitant dividends from their extravagant charges, the correct course was to get into negotiation with it, with a view to purchase. James Hogge, a Progressive, thought it was curious that some councillors expected a municipal cemetery to pay. The Conservative party maintained their club in St Leonard's at the ratepayers expense for 1d rate and they should not object to a similar rate for laying to rest people who would never trouble them again. The idea of a municipal cemetery had emanated from the Progressive Party, said James Inglis, and they had made a fetish of municipalisation, happy to spend ratepayer's money but buttoning their pockets if there was any suggestion that they should use their own. In the end the report was referred back to the Committee for further consideration by 17 votes to 14.[11]

On the new Council Cemetery Committee formed at the beginning of the next municipal year the forces were nearly equally balanced, seven Conservatives and six Progressives, but it was a matter of chance which party had the majority at its meetings, depending on who actually came. Three meetings were held before a revised report was formulated for the Council meeting on 6 March 1911 but at the last Davies and his supporters outnumbered the opposition. They had carefully reconsidered the report and had reduced the cost of works by £1,000 but this had little effect on the previously estimated ½d rate but it was thought this would diminish in years to come to less than ¼d. The City Surveyor had made test drillings at the wettest time of the year in the suggested site, three fields on the south side of Poppleton Road, adjacent to Beckfield Lane. On the higher ground, which was generally sandy, water was not found until a depth of ten feet had been reached. This seemed to meet the requirements of the Local Government Board for cemeteries – open porous soil on a site well elevated above the drainage level of the locality. In the lower field, however, water was reached at three feet so the City Surveyor was asked to negotiate for the purchase of the two higher fields only but the owners would only consider selling all the land, asking for £150 an acre. The Committee thus had no alternative but to recommend that the Council purchased all three fields. The political composition of the Council had not changed since the previous meeting so the same result was inevitable despite a rear-guard attempt to defer a decision until an expert had given advice on the possibility of contamination of the City's water supply.[12]

With the provision of the municipal cemetery now postponed once again Davies turned his efforts towards educating public opinion. He had written a pamphlet setting out the case for a municipal cemetery, published in September 1908, and he now contributed an article in a new series in the *Yorkshire Gazette* entitled *Towards a Progressive Policy* which appeared on 22 July 1911. The reduction of charges was, he said, the principal advantage of a municipal cemetery. York Public Cemetery Company paid a steady dividend of 10% to its shareholders, often with considerable bonuses. It reserved to itself the right to supply all stonework for public graves and protected itself from competition on private graves by charging 10s 0d for any work brought in by an outside mason. There were no cheap private graves similar to those provided in the majority of English cities. The only possibilities were either a second glass grave or a public grave. The first category, which could not be reserved for another member of the same family, was intended for six bodies and cost £1 15s. The only advantage was the opportunity of placing an inscription, not exceeding six lines, on the covering slab. Public graves cost from 6s 6d to 10s 6d depending on the rateable value of the house occupied by the deceased. Unless a person was willing to pay at least £3 15s he was obliged to bury his dead in a common grave, among the bodies of a number of strangers, however repugnant this may have been to his feelings. Two thirds of the interments in the cemetery were in this class, a higher proportion than elsewhere.

A cemetery under public control would be the means of breaking the monopoly enjoyed by the existing company, persons of the humblest means would have exclusive right of burial in what was virtually a private grave, stone masons would be able to compete freely for the provision of headstones and a large part of the city would have better access. Additionally it would be possible, at some time in the future, to provide a crematorium on the site. It had been argued that the cost was likely to exceed a 1d rate but even if no burials at all took place it would be only ½d. Thus a person living in a house of £20 rateable value would contribute about 1d a year towards what could be regarded as a mutual insurance scheme for reducing the cost of burial. The Progressive Party would make determined efforts to bring home to their opponents that the time was ripe for action to ensure that private interests making a dividend out of death no longer prevailed.[13]

Following the elections in 1911 the new Council, which was formed in November that year, no longer had an overall Conservative majority. Davies and his fellow Progressives had an opportunity to pursue their municipalisation policies with some hope of success. With the land in Poppleton judged to be not very suitable for a cemetery the Committee looked for another site on the south west of the City and entered into negotiations with M.J.O. Montagu, the owner of 24 acres in Knapton, three fields on either side of Knapton Lane which were part of the 65 acre Knapton Farm then occupied by William Mason who was giving up his tenancy in April 1914. After inspecting this land the Committee decided on 31 March 1913 to enter into an option to purchase it for £100 an acre but took the precaution of getting the tenant's agreement to allow trial bores to be made. After hearing the City Surveyor's report on 26 May the Committee decided to sign the option to purchase, its judgement apparently clouded by the need to realise its ambitions. A correspondent to the Yorkshire Herald, signing himself ACOMB, described the quicksands, water and other obstructions on the site `which surely should have been a check to the municipalising clique'. The newspaper sent a reporter to visit Knapton farm to see if these allegations were true but before he could write his article his newspaper received a second letter from ACOMB cataloguing the amount of water standing in each of the boreholes and test graves showing that the water table lay between 1ft 3ins and 5ft below the surface. The reporter was able to confirm ACOMB's observation and add comments made by a local farmer; `They could not have hit a worse place unless they wanted to make sure that those who were not dead before they were buried should be quietly drowned'. It was left to RATEPAYER in another letter to point out what this site would mean to the working classes in the way of expense -'a six mile journey, three out and three back'.[14]

In spite of the high cost of draining these three fields to lower the water table to ten feet the Committee estimated that the rate support for running a cemetery there would still not amount to more than ½d in the pound. Accordingly it recommended that the Council should purchase the land. Knowing that it was now likely that the Council would approve this recommendation Henry Rhodes Brown proposed at the meeting on 7 July that `before the Council decide on the provision of a municipal cemetery for York the matter be referred to the ratepayers to decide whether they will have such a cemetery'. His tactic, however, failed as his motion was ruled out of order by the Lord Mayor, Sir Joseph Sykes Rymer, a Conservative. Rhodes Brown's next delaying tactic was to propose, as an amendment to committee's recommendation, that the matter be deferred until January 1916, by which time every member of the Council, except the aldermen, would have had to stand for re-election. The citizens could then pick councillors who would represent them on the question of municipalisation. His proposal was defeated and the committee's recommendation was agreed by 20 votes to 18 with Alderman Joseph Agar, a trustee of the York Public Cemetery Company, abstaining.[15]

Even flushed with this success the Committee were not really satisfied with the Knapton fields and tried to find alternative sites. On 28 August 1913, after hearing from the City Surveyor the results of trial borings, it decided to make an offer of £100 an acre for 41 acres belonging to the Richardson Brothers, hay and straw dealers of Foss Islands Road, at the junction of Poppleton Road and Beckfield Lane. The Richardsons would not accept less than £145 an acre, considerably more than the price agreed with Montagu for his land. Nevertheless, having sought the Town Clerk's advice on the legal position of the contract with Montagu, it decided to ask the Council to rescind its earlier resolution to purchase the Knapton fields. This was agreed on 13 October and immediately contracts for the new sale were prepared but, before they could be signed, the Council elections restored the Conservative majority. Immediately seven councillors gave notice that they would be proposing a motion at the Council meeting on 17 November 'that the resolution passed by the Council on 13 October for the provision of a municipal cemetery be rescinded and no further action be taken at present, the recent election having emphatically decided against it.' The result was that the matter was referred back to the Cemetery Committee who, not daunted, repeated their recommendation at the Council meeting on 1 December. The councillors and aldermen then voted 22 to 20 to shelve the project, a result achieved by two councillors changing sides since the July vote and Alderman Agar exercising his vote on this occasion in spite of his vested interest. The Conservatives could be magnanimous in victory and decided to give the Richardson Brothers' solicitors £5 for their abortive costs, the final act in 19 years of discussion and prevarication.[16]

The debate in Council had been long and conducted on party political lines. The *Yorkshire Gazette* summed up the result in its leader column:

> The reactionaries in the City Council have got their way in the matter of the municipal cemetery, and the scheme has been shelved. We are convinced that the action of the newly obtained Conservative majority only means a postponement of the project. Sooner or later the municipal cemetery must be established. The only fear in regard to it is that if it is deferred much longer the cost of the establishment will be much increased, and the site will have to be at a still greater distance from the city. The latter consideration does not appear to have entered the minds of the opponents of the scheme,

whose only desire seemed to be to get rid of it without any regard for the future. Nothing new was brought out in the discussion, which, for so grave a subject, was of a really entertaining character.

There was Councillor Bury, for instance. Much practice in the art of public speaking has given the new member for Monk Ward a ready wit – perhaps a readier tongue. He charged the Progressive Party with thinking more about the dead than the living. It sounded very fine given with due emphasis, and elicited quite a chorus of approval from the Tory benches. Unfortunately for the argument, however, it is a fact, as pointed out by Councillor Davies, that it is not the dead who pay burial fees, but the living. Not long ago an earnest opponent of the scheme told the Council that he knew the minds of the poor people in the graves as he had been amongst them. From this, and the statement made by Councillor Bury, it might be inferred that the dead people had some interest in the cost of burial, and that the Progressive Party were anxious that that interest should not be disturbing to them. But the burden of death is always upon the living, and, for the great majority of people, this burden is added to by the horrible thought that high dividends are being earned by a few individuals out of – death![17]

The Conservatives obviously had no intention of considering the matter again while they had control of the Council and decided on 9 November 1914 that the Cemetery Committee would not be re-appointed for the next municipal year, the effective end of the municipalisation debate.[18] In fact the Council eventually became the owners of a cemetery by no deliberate action on its part. In 1937 Dringhouses was brought within the City boundary and with it came a small public cemetery which had been opened in 1927 on a triangular site, between the railway at Challoner's Winn and the Tadcaster Road, given by Colonel Eason Wilkinson, the Lord of the Manor. It was just over one acre in extent and had space for only 765 graves. After having reserved it in 1942 for only the residents of the ecclesiastical parish of Dringhouses the Council decided, three years later, to extend it by an extra 16 acres using five fields on the York side. The first plan, approved in March 1948, would have provided sufficient graves for 98 years at a cost of £122,800 but the Ministry of Health would only consider a scheme that would meet the burial requirements of the district for five years. Consequently a modified plan, costing only £11,000 was prepared instead and was consecrated by the Bishop of Selby, C.F. Knyvett, on 12 August 1958. Further extensions were planned but the land was eventually made available for Tesco supermarket and car park. New sites at the junction of Askham Lane and Moor Lane, on Clifton Aerodrome and between Sim Balk Lane and Bishopthorpe Road were also considered but the opening of York Crematorium in Bishopthorpe Road on 11 April 1962 and an agreement reached in 1969 with Fulford Parish Council, preserving burial rights for York citizens in Fulford cemetery, (opened 1915), for the next 50 years, put paid to any further thoughts of a municipal cemetery and ended another stage in the saga of a municipal cemetery for the City.[19]

Burial, as a method of disposal of the dead, is now very much in the minority. Since 1987 70% of the people dying in England and Wales have been cremated, a triumph for the Cremation Society of England, formed in 1874 to promote this alternative to burial, which it believed would prevent premature burial, reduce the expense of funerals and spare mourners the necessity of standing exposed to the weather during interment. Cremation would be a `necessary sanitary precaution against the propagation of disease among a population growing larger in relation to the area it occupied' and the ashes, kept in urns in columbaria, would be safe from vandalism. At the first meeting of the Society on 13 January 1874 the members declared their disapproval of: -

> the present custom of burying the dead, and we desire to substitute some mode which shall rapidly resolve the body into its component elements, by a process which cannot offend the living, and shall render the remains perfectly innocuous. Until some better method is devised we desire to adopt that usually known as cremation.

An acre of land at Woking was bought from the London Necropolis Company and a furnace was installed there in which the body of a horse was completely and rapidly reduced to ashes on 17 March 1879. Local opposition prevented the building being used for its intended purpose until 26 March 1885 when Mrs Pickersgill was the first to be cremated there, but not the first in this country. In 1882 the Society had been unable to comply with the request of Captain Hanham of Blandford to cremate two members of his family so he erected a crematorium on his own estate where he disposed of the bodies of his wife and mother on 8 and 9 October and where he was himself cremated a year later.[20]

York was introduced to the concept of cremation on 15 February 1881 by H. E. Spencer, a surgeon at York Dispensary, who delivered a lecture at the York Institute entitled `Burial and Cremation'. He concluded by saying: -

But when every care is taken [in burying a body] the fact remains that these arrangements can in their nature be only of a temporary character, if the population continue to increase, and peace prevail. Our comparatively modern extramural cemetery for this city has already become nearly surrounded by a dense population. Go where you will, you see the same thing. You may make an extramural cemetery, but you cannot keep it so. And though there is perhaps no great urgency just yet for enquiring what is to be done next, that enquiry must inevitably be made if not by our children, at least by our children's children.[21]

Cremation became available for the citizens of York when Hull opened the first municipal crematorium in the United Kingdom in 1901. In Yorkshire this was followed by the installation of a Toisoul Fradet Gas Oven at Lawnswood Crematorium at Leeds in 1905. Another British first was achieved by Harrogate in 1936 when it opened its electric cremator. The first cremated remains to be interred in York cemetery were those of a member of a local family sent up from Golders Green Crematorium. Next came ashes from Manchester in 1909 and from San Francisco, USA, in 1912. In 1962, as has already been related, York got its own municipal crematorium where, between May 1986 and May 1987, York undertakers took 1,643 bodies for disposal – contrasting dramatically with six burials at Dringhouses Burial Ground and 35 at York Cemetery.

Thus in 1913 York Public Cemetery Company was no longer threatened by opposition from a municipal cemetery. Cremation, not to be used for more than 1% of deaths until 1932, was having a negligible effect on their business. The trustees, however, were aware that their cemetery was a finite asset with only limited opportunity for expansion and must eventually run out of space for burial. Another factor which may have pleased them personally but must have concerned them as businessmen was the improvement in public health and the consequent falling death rate. When the cemetery was opened in 1837 the death rate in York was 23 per 1000 population. This was to fall only gradually in subsequent years but occasionally the number of deaths in a year fell below the average. When this happened the shareholders at the annual general meeting were informed that this must be gratifying to them, though not to their pecuniary advantage and, perhaps with tongue in cheek, the Board of Health was congratulated on the sanitary health of the City.[22] The falling death rate was more than compensated for by an increasing population and the peak in the 19th century was reached in 1891 with 1,446 burials in that year. Soon afterwards, coinciding with the installation of the first comprehensive sewage system in the City and the opening of the treatment works at Naburn in 1895, the death rate, then at 18 per 1000, started to fall more rapidly reaching 13 per 1000 by the First World War. With it the number of burials also fell, not to be balanced by the still rising population until the 1920s but by then other factors, cremation and burial elsewhere, were beginning to affect the business of the company – the writing was clearly on the wall!

NOTES

1. *York Herald*, 9 February 1856.
2. YCA BC 17/4 p 62.
3. *Yorkshire Gazette*, 3 August 1878.
4. YCM 1893/4, pp 119, 120, 186 & 242.
5. YCM 1893/4 p 235; YCM 1896/7 pp 532 & 637; YCM 1899/1900 p 154; YCM 1900/1 pp 514 & 732; YCA BC19/2 p 144.
6. YCA BC46 6 December 1901, 20 March & 27 November 1902; YCM 1902/3 pp 755/6; YCM 1903/4 p 124; YCM 1904/5 pp 102/ 3 & 213.
7. C.H. Feinstein (ed.) *York 1831-1981*, R. I. Hills, 'The City Council and Electoral Politics, 1901-1971', p 259.
8. YCM 1907/8 p 605; YCM 1908/9 p 1095.
9. YCA BC46 2 December 1909, 17 March & 8 September 1910.
10. YCM 1909/10 pp 1339-1343; *Yorkshire Gazette* 5 November 1910.
11. YCM 1909/10 pp 1440/1; *Yorkshire Gazette* 19 November 1910.
12. YCA BC46 16 January & 17 February 1911; YCM 1910/11 pp 362/4. 407/8.
13. *Yorkshire Gazette*, 22 July 1911.
14. YCA BC46 31 March, 14 April & 26 May 1913; *Yorkshire Herald*, 30 & 31 May 1913.
15. YCM 1912/13 pp 786/9 & 964/5.
16. YCA BC46 28 August, 19 & 29 September; YCM 1912/13 pp 1161, 1249/50, 1330 & 1371/2; YCM 1913/14 pp 98/9.
17. *Yorkshire Gazette*, 6 December 1913.
18. YCM 1913/14 p 1163.
19. *Yorkshire Herald*, 26 Feb 1927; YCM 1941/2 p 652; YCM 1947/48/49 p 420; *Yorkshire Evening Press*, 11 August 1958, 23 January 1963, 10 January 1975.
20. The Cremation Society of Great Britain *The History of Modern Cremation in Great Britain from 1874* (1974) p 65.
21. H.E. Spencer *Burial and Cremation* (1881) p 9.
22. *Yorkshire Gazette*, 3 August 1867, 10 July 1880.

5: 'To Dust Returneth' – Decline

Life is real! Life is earnest!
And the grave is not its goal;
Dust thou art, to dust returneth,
Was not spoken of the soul.

H.W Longfellow A Psalm of Life

As the Edwardian era was drawing to a close the York Public Cemetery Company lost two of its principal employees. First Thomas Brown was succeeded as superintendent on 2 July 1908 by Harry Robertson, who had been engaged on 1 December the previous year, and then on 8 May 1909 the chaplain, the Revd A.B. Armstrong, died at the early age of 53 to be replaced by the Revd Edward Charnock Smith, then Rector of All Saints, Pavement and of St Saviour's from 1911, at the same salary of £100 a year.[1] In January 1913 when William John Hands died further changes were necessary. Joseph Agar now found himself the sole survivor of the trustees appointed in 1868. He was aged 80 and it was imperative that some new ones were appointed to avoid the legal complications his executors would face if he died in sole possession of the company's assets. At the annual general meeting in June 1914 nine new trustees were elected to join Joseph Agar, an election which, according to clause 39 of the Deed of Settlement, should have taken place in 1885 when, on the death of Michael Varvill, the number of trustees was reduced to six.[2] After the election the new trustees were:

Joseph Agar, Currier
James Ramsay, Medical Practitioner
Thomas Lund
Thomas Dennett, Joiner
William Seale, Brushmaker
James Melrose, Brewer
George Wood, Farmer
Thomas Stamp, Bookkeeper
Joseph Puckering
James Knowlson

One of the first tasks of the new superintendent was to recommend some increases in the scale of burial charges, which, apart from some additions to cater for the second class graves of 1848, the larger London Burial Board grave size introduced in 1857, and an extra 6s 6d category of poor burials in 1870, had remained the same since the cemetery opened in 1837. In the same period the cost of living had nearly doubled and, even if the profits of the stone-yard were still sufficient to cover the continuing loss on the burial account, something had to be done if the shareholders were to continue to be paid a bonus in addition to their regular 10% dividend.

In 1910 the three categories of poor burials and the cost of burial in a second class grave were left unchanged but a graduated scale of charges was introduced for the purchase of private grave plots in both the original area of the cemetery and in the new ground. The increases were, to an extent, hidden by the original prices being retained and new lower prices being introduced as well as higher charges for the better plots (figure i).[3] At about the same time the wording on the grave certificates was altered from `These are to certify that the Grave Numbered …… in the York Public Cemetery or Burial Ground is the Property of ……' to 'These are to certify that all rights of Burial in the Grave Numbered …… in the York Public Cemetery or Burial Ground belong to …….' This was an attempt to solve another problem – the eventual filling of the cemetery. If the cemetery company had continued to dispose of ownership of the grave plots the day would eventually be reached when it no longer owned any of its burial ground but would still have a contractual obligation, under the terms of its agreements with individual families, to maintain it and their graves with no income other than an annual maintenance payment or the interest accruing on a single lump sum payment. By giving right of burial only the company could continue to own the freehold and perhaps, at a later date, reuse the graves, especially as the occupancy of private graves was not as high as the company had hoped. The London Burial Board rules allowed a grave to be reopened for a non family burial 14 years after the previous adult interment. In this period of time, under normal conditions, a body would be totally decomposed and the grave could be then used many times before it was so full of bones to make it unfit for further use.[4]

Figure i

	1837	1910
Original Area 7½x3ft		£2 15s 0d
	£3 15s 0d	£3 15s 0d
		£4 15s 0d
New Ground 9x4ft		£4 4s 0d
	£5 5s 0d	£5 5s 0d
		£6 6s 0d
		£7 7s 0d

The declaration of war in 1914 brought rapid inflation in its wake and the company found it necessary to review its charges, both during the war and in 1921, after the cessation of hostilities when prices had risen to three times their pre-war level. On both these occasions the charges for private graves were left unchanged and the increases applied only to the most prolific burials, those in public and second class graves (figure ii). The second increase, like the first, had the immediate benefit of turning the loss on the interment account into a reasonable profit which, coupled with the continuing profit on the stone-yard account, increased the shareholder's annual return from 10% plus 5s 0d bonus (12.5%) to 10% plus 10s 0d bonus (15%) in 1922 but not in 1923 when some of the new profits were invested in 5% War Loan 1929-47 stock (figure iii).[5]

Figure ii   Public Burials

	1837	1848	1870	1910	During War	1921
Occupants of houses						
Under £5 rateable value	4s 6d		4s 6d	6s 6d		
Under £10 rateable value			6s 6d	7s 6d	17s 6d	£1 7s 6d
All others	10s 6d		10s 6d	l0s 6d		
Second Class Grave			£1 15s 0d		£2 5s 0d	£2 15s 0d

Figure iii	Interment Account Profit/Loss	Stone-yard Account Profit/Loss	Combined Profit	Number of Burials	Dividend
	£ s d	£ s d	£ s d		
1919	+888 9 8	+ 635 8 6	+1523 18 2	1419	not known
1920	-219 6 4	+ 924 11 2	+ 705 4 10	995	10% + 5s
1921	-166 3 8	+1548 2 11	+1381 19 3	955	10% + 5s
1922	+527 6 9	+1158 19 7	+1786 6 4	1077	10% +10s
1923	+511 6 9	+1241 11 1	+1752 17 10	855	10%

During the First World War York contained the Headquarters of Northern Command, the York Record Office, the Depot of the West Yorkshire Regiment and four auxiliary hospitals. Because of this military presence in the City 146

The funeral procession of Private Michael Killoran of the 1st East Riding Regiment approaching the cemetery on 17 February 1912, watched by the sphinx on its pillar at the southern end of the boundary fence. The trees were later replaced by poplars which were, in turn, removed in 1961 because they were said to be dangerous.

[Photograph courtesy of Felicity Stasiak]

members of the Imperial Forces were buried in 143 graves in the cemetery. Some, having been brought back from the front to the York hospitals for treatment of their wounds or for the effects of gas, unfortunately succumbed while others, holding administrative posts in the York garrison died from natural causes and one, Sergeant Edward Gordon Beckett RFA, was killed in a Zeppelin raid on York on 2 May 1916. Worker Nellie Whitworth of Queen Mary's Army Auxiliary Corps who was attached to No 2 Infantry Records Office, the only female of the 146, died on 21 October 1918 of sickness at the age of 26. Others, killed in training accidents or dying at depots away from York, were brought back home for burial. Two other people bring the total of war burials in the cemetery up to 148, a German soldier and an Austrian civilian, both detained in a prisoner of war camp near York. They were Anton Ruff, died 14 October, and Agust Burkert, died 16 October 1914, buried together in a public grave.

FUNERAL OF THE LATE ALDERMAN LANCELOT FOSTER, ENTERING YORK CEMETARY. 1.

The horse drawn hearse carrying the body of Alderman Lancelot Foster enters the cemetery on 21 June 1913. The accompanying procession had walked to the cemetery from his house in Bootham.

The Imperial War Graves Commission was founded by Royal Charter on 21 May 1917 to be responsible for the care and maintenance of cemeteries as well as the graves and memorials, not only in special War cemeteries but wherever situated, of the officers and men of the naval, military and air forces of His Majesty, who had fallen in the war. The period covered was eventually defined as 1914 to 1921. Of the 143 war graves in the cemetery only 89 were marked by the Commission, first with small wooden crosses and later, after 1924, by its standard headstones of Portland stone with a curved top, carved with a unit badge and a simple inscription recording the name, rank, number and dates of the person buried there. 60 graves had private memorials provided by the families of the deceased, including eight graves which have Commission memorials as well. Five graves were not marked. There are 107 other war graves at Fulford Cemetery, in the military section, opened on 27 October 1915.[6]

The body of Band Sergeant William John Cochrane of the Royal Scots Greys was brought to the cemetery on 24 June 1913 in a coffin carried on a gun limber. It was preceded by a horse with reversed boots in the stirrups. A tramcar in Fulford Road had to wait until the procession had passed completely into Cemetery Road.

[Photograph courtesy of Felicity Stasiak]

Towards the end of the war York experienced the effects of an influenza epidemic that had spread through Europe, America and India, its progress helped by the movements of troops throughout these areas. There was a comparatively mild epidemic between 1 and 27 July 1918 in which 33 York residents succumbed but, in a much more severe outbreak between 5 October 1918 and 11 January 1919, the number of deaths reached 322 – 267 citizens and 55 military personnel. The peak of the epidemic was reached between 20 October and 23 November when there were 203 civilian deaths in the City. This imposed a great strain on the cemetery staff. During the nine days up to 31 October there were 110 burials in the cemetery against a normally expected figure of 30 for the same period in previous years. To cope with this abnormal demand the superintendent had to ask the military authorities to send some soldiers to help with the grave digging. On 23 July, during the first epidemic, M. Theakston of 57 St Paul's Terrace wrote to the *Yorkshire Herald* to complain of the state of the cemetery. He had been unable to find the graves of his relatives because of the length of the grass growing over and around them. Whether or not this was a temporary lapse due to the extra work occasioned by the epidemic is not known but he also complained of the state of the paths and suggested that when they were put in order the company should provide a rubber-tyred carrier to take coffins from the chapel to the grave-side.[7]

The floral tributes round the grave of Band Sergeant Cochrane included, at the right hand end, a large wreath, in the shape of a harp, from his colleagues in the band.

[Photograph courtesy of Felicity Stasiak]

The cemetery was gradually filling up. Burial had started in 1910 on the land purchased from Joseph Agar in 1877 (section B) although it had not been nor never was to be consecrated. All that remained for future use was the Wheatsheaf field, 2¼ acres purchased from the executors of William Reaston of Thorganby in 1878. It had been approved as a burial ground on 26 March 1877 at a time when there were no houses in Cemetery Road near it. A terrace had since been built in this road opposite the western end of the land and it appeared that there might be objections from the occupants under the Burial Act 1855 which contained

George William Jackson started work at the cemetery on 21 February 1920 at the age of 23. When he retired 47 years later, on 21 May 1966, he had risen to the post of cemetery foreman. He died on 2 March 1980 and is buried in the cemetery.

[Photograph courtesy of Mrs. Alma Winship]

a provision that no ground not already used or appropriated for a cemetery should be used for burials without the consent of the owner, lessee or occupier of any house within 100 yards of it. The company decided in 1912 to seek a legal opinion from a barrister, Wilfrid Gutch of Lincoln's Inn, son of John James Gutch of Holgate Lodge who had once been one of the company's secretaries. The matter was complicated by the company's status. Wilfrid Gutch was of the opinion that it was not an illegal company as it had been formed before the Companies Act 1862 but it was a quasi-corporation or partnership of numerous individuals possessing real estate. By conveying its land to trustees the company had got over any difficulties under the Statute of Mortmain 1279 which would have prevented it buying or selling land without royal licence. He saw nothing in its Deed of Settlement to suggest that it was carrying on its business under the Burial Acts and, consequently, it was not necessary for it to get the consent of owners of property built either before or after the company appropriated its land for burials. The only liability was for Common Law nuisance.[8]

Having established the legal position the company did not make any attempt to use the Wheatsheaf field until 1923 when it decided to lay it out as a park (Section C) and asked Backhouse Nurseries to prepare a scheme. The design finally agreed involved draining and levelling the field and laying it out with a central avenue along its length which was intersected by four paths at right angles leading to the serpentine walks which ran along the boundary. It was screened from Joseph Agar's house by a shrubbery and trees along its southern boundary and from Section B to the east by a rustic trellis and pergola made with native larch still covered with bark on which rambler roses would be trained. The eastern end of the bank running along the boundary with the original cemetery was to be made into a rockery of Horsforth stone and planted with a very good collection of Alpine plants. A semi-circular carriage drive was to be constructed connecting two gateways on Cemetery Road. The road boundary was to be fenced with iron railings. The whole area was to be turfed to form a lawn which had ten flowerbeds let into it, planted out with 78 specimen trees and shrubs. The work was completed by September 1924 and cost £2,584 1s 1d (figure iv). The Lawn Park area, as it

Figure iv	Construction Costs - Lawn Park Section C			
		£	s	d
Backhouse Nurseries - Laying out, draining and planting		2198	4	7
Leo. Woodcock - Erection of wall and fixing concrete coping		90	0	0
Messrs. Bushell - Supplying iron gates and railings		177	8	0
Concrete Ltd. - Supplying concrete for coping		72	10	0
Messrs. Tindall - Laying on water		131	8	6
York Corporation - Making 2 crossings in Cemetery Road footpath		32	0	0
	Total	2584	1	1

was to be known, was consecrated by the Bishop of Whitby, the Rt. Revd H.StJ.S Woollcombe, on 3 October and the first burial was made in it on 13 November 1925.[9] To ensure it remained as a park and to make grass cutting easy special regulations were made: -

In the Park section no glass or artificial wreaths or shades are allowed, all receptacles for cut flowers must be sunk level with the earth, a small number plate will be fitted into the mound when completed and no other identification mark is permitted except the usual monumental mark. Jam jars and flower holders of a similar objectionable type will be removed.[10]

The provision of a lawn park section had perhaps been suggested by the Imperial War Graves Commission who wanted to erect a Cross of Sacrifice in the cemetery to mark its status as a war cemetery. On 2 April 1924 it was agreed that for the sum of £150 the company would grant the Commission the exclusive right of

The Lawn Park section in the early 1930s, looking towards Cemetery Road and the Cross of Sacrific, showing the neatly clipped lawns and formal tree-lined paths and hedges.

[Photograph courtesy of Mrs. Alma Winship]

'erecting, placing and maintaining ...... for ever' a cross on a site in the projected park section where the central avenue intersected with one of the cross paths. The area round the cross was to be planted with grass or with shrubs and flowers and all reasonable precautions were to be taken to ensure that the monument should not be wilfully damaged or destroyed. The Imperial War Graves Commission, in 1919, had asked the architect, Sir Reginald Theodore Blomfield (1856-1942) to design a Cross of Sacrifice which could be erected at cemeteries in England and it proposed to erect his type A cross in York Cemetery, one of some 40 chosen for this privilege. Fulford cemetery was also to have a similar cross but as there were more war dead buried in York Cemetery the cross there was to be 20 feet high, five feet higher than that at Fulford. It was constructed of Stancliffe sandstone from Darley Dale in Derbyshire with two bronze swords fixed on the stem. The base was inscribed; -

> To the Glory of God and the honoured memory of those sailors and soldiers who gave their lives for the country in the Great War, 1914-1918, and who lie buried in this cemetery.

The view of the Lawn Park section looking east shows one of the less formal serpentine paths and the shrubberies on its boundary. While it still had a park-like appearance in the early 1930s it is now completely covered with graves.

[Photograph courtesy of Mrs. Alma Winship]

It was unveiled on 28 May 1925 by Lt General Sir Charles Harington, GOC Northern Command, at a ceremony attended by trustees of the cemetery company and representatives of the Yorkshire regiments and the Imperial War Grave Commission with music provided by the band of the Border Regiment.

Sir Charles said that since the war there had been signs of forgetfulness of the men who had withstood the onslaught of the German Army and they could never call themselves Englishmen and Yorkshiremen if they forgot the sacrifice of the men buried in York Cemetery. The dedication was performed by the Revd W.D. Hughes, acting Assistant Chaplain General of Northern Command. The Yorkshire Gazette commented that 'the cross had been erected in the most beautiful part of the cemetery and with nature seen at her best there was a picturesque setting for the unveiling ceremony'.[11]

Despite the opening of the lawn park section with an additional 2¼ acres of burial space the superintendent, Harry Robertson, was worried about his own and the cemetery's future. He made a report to the trustees at the end of the company's

1925/6 financial year recommending that it was urgent that it should be made into a limited liability company and that he should be provided with a superannuation scheme. He thought that the number of grave spaces still available would only last for ten to twelve years and that the trustees were thus confronted with two alternatives; to wind up the company when it died a natural death or to acquire fresh land to enable it to carry on its operations. To realise the first alternative the share capital of £6,000 would have to be refunded but the company's cash assets at this time amounted to £8,164. Profits in the few years remaining to the company could be allocated to a special fund to be used for the upkeep of the cemetery as an open space when it was no longer available for burials.

The only new land adjacent to the cemetery to fulfil his second alternative belonged to Joseph Agar, a cemetery trustee. If this could be acquired it would prolong the life of the cemetery by another seven years but as it would be difficult to drain it could only be used for the cheaper graves. It was possible that a new cemetery could be opened in another part of the City but it would have to be within two miles of the City centre and served by a tram route. If such land could be found a crematorium could be built on it which would not provide any return on capital for some years but the company would be first in the field and ready when cremation became the general practice. With careful management the new and the old cemeteries, working together, would enable the York Public Cemetery Company to retain the greater part of burial and monumental work in the City and still pay a dividend to its shareholders.[12]

Having twice previously allowed their numbers to fall below the defined minimum the trustees surprisingly failed to appoint any new ones until 1920 when the brewer, John Joseph Hunt was elected to join the three survivors, James Melrose, Joseph Puckering and William Seale, but they were still two short of the required number of six. Three more, Joseph Agar, Geoffrey Herbert Swift and James Frederick Bushell, elected in 1924, took the number to seven and then, in 1929, acting correctly for the first time, after the deaths of James Melrose in his 101st year and Joseph Puckering, the number was raised to nine[13]:-

William Seale. Brushmaker
John Joseph Hunt. Brewer
Joseph Agar. Leather Merchant
Geoffrey Herbert Swift, Solicitor
James Frederick Bushell, Agricultural Instrument Maker
Ignatius Warner

Samuel Arthur Fowler
George Ernest Garbutt, Saddler
Herbert Leeds Swift, Solicitor

But before the four new trustees could join their deliberations four of the other five entered into an agreement with the fifth, Joseph Agar, to buy a field, used as allotments and measuring 2¾ acres, between Kilburn House, his family home for three generations, which he was also selling, and the cemetery, a recommendation made by the superintendent five years previously. Before the deal could be completed they had to find out if they were empowered to purchase land and if the Ministry of Health would approve its use as a burial ground. Formal approval was not given until 15 August 1929 but when Wilfrid Gutch gave his opinion on the first matter on 11 June it was known that the Ministry had no objections. The Deed of Settlement did not contain powers to purchase land but Gutch had no doubts that the trustees could do so if the land was essential to the company's existence and undertaking. As five years of the estimated ten to twelve years of further life for the cemetery had elapsed there could be no doubt that this purchase was essential! In asking for this opinion the trustees cannot have been aware of, or were not sure of, the legality of the five similar purchases that had been made by their predecessors between 1848 and 1878.

Joseph Agar received £1,360 (£500 an acre) for his field and it was conveyed to the trustees on 6 September. The new owners of Kilburn House had no objection to the field being used as a burial ground. Continuing the park theme the design for the new area (section D) included at the western end a formal lily pond, filled in and used for burial from November 1951 when extra grave spaces were required, but certainly there when The Most Revd William Temple, Archbishop of York, consecrated this section on 6 May 1931. An indication that this new ground was essential to the company's existence and undertaking was that on 15 May, only 9 days after consecration, the first burial was made in it.[14] One unforeseen consequence of this latest extension to the cemetery was the cutting off of the water supply to the Piking Well on New Walk as it appeared that the spring feeding it was a cemetery drain or at least was getting some of its water from the drain laid to the cemetery in 1867!

James Melrose, who died before this extension to the cemetery was purchased, had been a very active participant in many City institutions, the cemetery company included, right to the end of his very long life. He must have been very gratified to see the successful interment of Eliza Jane Hands in her family vault under the portico of the cemetery chapel on 21 September 1928 shortly after his hundredth birthday. In 1840 Thomas Hands, one of the original trustees, exercising his right as a shareholder, had purchased a vault for five bodies under the portico of the cemetery chapel. It was first used for his wife, Mary, in 1860, followed by his daughter-in-law, Jane, wife of his son, William John, in 1863. Eleven years later, in 1874, he was laid to rest in his family vault and it was to be 39 years before it was used again; this time, on 23 January 1913, for William John. On the night before this interment his son, Arthur William Hands, was shown a telegram that the undertaker had received from the cemetery superintendent saying there was only room for one in the vault and, on checking after the funeral, found that the space remaining would require the fifth and final coffin to be less than 20 inches in depth. This, in the opinion of Harry Robertson, was not sufficient for a further burial. On learning this, his mother Eliza Jane, the second wife of William John Hands, was much upset, as it was her wish that she be buried with her husband.

On the suggestion of his mother Arthur Hands wrote to James Melrose, an old friend of his father, asking, if he was acquainted with the chairman of the cemetery, could he arrange a meeting between the family and the company. Arthur Hands must have been very gratified to find that he had, in fact, written to the chairman himself. James Melrose replied that he had told the cemetery committee that he wanted to do everything possible to comply with the family's wishes 'as if your late father had been my near relative'. With this directive the committee agreed that a fifth coffin could be put in the vault provided that it was less than 18 inches deep and that the vault was hermetically sealed under 3 inches of concrete and a stone slab 1¼ inches thick. After the death of his mother on 17 September 1928 Arthur Hands wrote to inform the superintendent that he would be bringing his mother's body to the cemetery for a funeral on the afternoon of 21 September in a coffin that was only 16 inches deep. This brought the response that the cemetery committee would prefer the interment to be made in the morning as this would enable the funeral to be kept as private as possible; in other words they had reasons for not wanting anyone else to see the special arrangements that had been made for what was to be the last interment in the portico vaults.[16]

The other seed sown by Harry Robertson in his 1926 report took longer to germinate. In June 1931 the company secretary became aware that a resolution was to be made at the annual general meeting, to be held on 27 July, proposing that £6,000 should be taken from the reserve fund of £10,531 and distributed to the shareholders as a 100% dividend, in effect a full repayment of the face value of the shares whose market value was then between £12 and £14. In writing to Wilfrid Gutch for yet another legal opinion the company informed him that it now thought that the cemetery would be used up within the next twenty years and that the successful monumental business, worked up by Harry Robertson, on which the company was dependent for a large part of its income, would be likely to die with him when he retired or at the best gradually fade away. It also wanted to consider the benefits of its becoming a limited liability company. Gutch advised on 23 July that the proprietors were indeed competent to declare a 100% dividend paid from a fund of accumulated profits. As this would have the effect of writing off the cemetery extension account they should first consider what the present commitments and liabilities were. Was there any possibility that additional land could be acquired? What was the contractual liability to the purchasers of graves? In the event of the cemetery closing sufficient funds should be kept to keep it in decent order and its walls and fences in repair. If the burials had been properly made there was very little risk of any nuisance being caused except, possibly, the contamination of water by percolation but a serious liability would be incurred if a road was later built against one of the long boundaries of the cemetery.

Kenneth Sissons, who died on 13 August 1928 and was buried in the cemetery three days later, in 'perpetual sleep'. While it was a custom in Victorian times to photograph dead bodies before committing them to the grave it is unusual to find examples of this practice at this date.

[Photograph - Florence Hanstock]

There was no problem in converting the company into a limited liability company under the Companies Act 1929. The benefit would be that the company and its shareholders would carry on the business under Articles of Association embodying provisions similar to those in the 1838 Deed of Settlement but would have their liability limited to the amount of its assets and their shareholding. If this step was taken and, at a later time, with no income for its upkeep the cemetery became a nuisance, there was the possibility that someone could obtain a judgement against the company resulting in it being wound up as well as being severely criticised in the local press for having allowed such an old established and sound financial corporation to come to such a pass. Wilfrid Gutch saw no ground at all for the conclusion that an equally competent manager could not be found to succeed Harry Robertson or that the monumental business and its goodwill would fail until a few years after the cemetery was full.[17]

This reply concentrated the minds of the trustees on the possibility of becoming a limited liability company and they sought further explanations from Wilfrid Gutch in November 1931. To take this step a resolution would have to be made at an annual or extraordinary general meeting. If such a company was then formed the contractual liability of the company to grave owners who had paid a sum of money to have their graves kept in order in perpetuity would remain the same although now limited in extent. When the cemetery was full this liability would remain but there would only be a moral obligation to keep the rest of the cemetery in a tidy condition. Looking further ahead, if the company was wound up the liquidator would have to keep sufficient funds to meet these liabilities before the company's assets were distributed to the shareholders. In answer to a direct question on the advisability of turning the York Public Cemetery Company into a limited liability company Gutch replied that the only advantage would be, if the company was liquidated, that the shareholders would escape any further payments, as also would the liquidator after six years. On the other hand there could be benefits in forming the successful monumental business into a separate company to free its profits from contributing to the reserve fund to meet the liabilities of the cemetery.[18]

Even with this additional information nothing was done to alter the status of the company which, while operating efficiently on a day to day basis under the management of Harry Robertson, seems to have lacked direction at the policy making level. Earlier in 1931 the trustees had to sort out another muddle their lack of attention had got them into. Their investments in 5% War Stock 1929/47 had been made in the names of James Melrose, Joseph Agar and Herbert Leeds Swift. Swift was the last survivor of the three and on his death on 11 October 1930 his executors became the effective owners of the investment and special arrangements had to be made with the Stock Exchange to reregister the stock in the names of another group of trustees.[19]

The Salvation Army Band heads the funeral procession of a John William Smallwood, a Citadel comrade who died on 24 January 1934, as it passes over Castle Mills Bridge in the rain on its way to the cemetery.

[Photograph courtesy of the York Corps]

The Corporation as always, was watching the cemetery company carefully to ensure that the citizens of York were not disadvantaged by any of its activities and occasionally it made what it considered to be helpful suggestions. In February 1932 Alderman William Horsman who lived at 23 Heslington Road persuaded the Council that great benefit would accrue to the residents of Heworth, Tang Hall, Hull Road and the Heslington Road area if visitors could be allowed to use the gate into the cemetery in Belle Vue Terrace. The Streets and Buildings Committee was asked to send a deputation to negotiate with the company but the Corporation was rebuffed with a response from the company that it was of the opinion that the interests of the public and the grave space owners would be best served by the entrances remaining as at present. The members of the corporation cannot have been too pleased when the company raised its prices in the same year against a general trend of prices which had fallen steadily since the years immediately after the war. While interments in second class graves were left at the same price those in the still popular public graves were raised to £1 10s 0d. No longer were small grave plots offered in the original part of the cemetery but the cost of larger plots now ranged from £3 3s 0d (a slightly reduced minimum price) to £12 12s 0d (a considerably increased maximum price). These increases were presumably made to restore the ailing burial account to a reasonable profit. If this was so it certainly succeeded as by 1936 the profit was £1,029 7s 9d and reached a peak of £1,404 6s 7d the next year.[21]

George Jackson, in 1933, mowing a lawn under the shadow of the Twelve Apostles, the poplar trees, which shortly after he had started work in the cemetery, he had carried in under his arm to plant on the boundary between Sections C and D.

[Photograph courtesy of Mrs. Alma Winship]

By the beginning of 1934 the company had decided that, with only a limited life left for the burial business, it should now take whatever action was necessary to separate the stone-yard business from the liability to maintain the graves and the cemetery and, at the same time, distribute some of the accumulated reserve fund which was now standing at £14,500, mostly invested in Government stocks. A new company, to be called the York Memorial Company, was to be formed and capitalised from the reserve fund and both it and the old company registered under the Companies Act 1929. The cemetery company proposed to send a letter to all its shareholders advising them of its proposals but, before it did, it asked Wilfrid Gutch once again for an opinion. His response on 15 March was that the letter to the shareholders was inadequate. If the company wished to make the changes it proposed it would have to seek authority at a general meeting to amend or add new clauses to the Deed of Settlement. He thought that it would have tax advantages to the shareholders, avoiding the liability to both income and surtax, if, after the formation of the York Memorial Company, its capital was distributed to them as shares in the new company. Gutch also advised the company to seek advice as to the most economical method of achieving its objectives and it may have been the result of getting this advice, or the new profitability of the burial account or perhaps the prospect of getting more land that convinced the company that it should not pursue its plans at this time.[22]

In 1936, with the reserve fund increased to £18,450 the company wrote off £6,000, the cost of the old cemetery and recommended a dividend of 10% plus a bonus of £1 (20%), both free from Income Tax which was paid by the company. To further the business of the stone-yard a new show room, costing £387 10s 0d, was built just inside the cemetery on the opposite side of the main gate from the lodge and in the next year extensive alterations were made to the office, which, when they were completed in 1938, had cost £505 14s 3d. The annual general meeting held on 28 July 1937 was the hundredth and a number of comparisons were made with the first in 1838. Then the excess of receipts over expenditure had been £21 5s 9d and the rates paid on an eight acre cemetery were less than £10. Now 100 years later the equivalent figures were £4,917 and rates of £227 on 23¼ acres, a fairly rosy picture but the underlying problems still had to be faced. Continuity with the opening of the cemetery was maintained by Joseph Agar who had succeeded his father, Joseph Agar, who had in turn followed his father, Benjamin Agar, who had been an original trustee. The first solicitors had been William Slater, who had died soon afterwards, and the firm of Blanchard and Richardson which had been absorbed into Cowling and Swift, the solicitors at the centenary. There had only been five superintendents. On the other hand there had been 10 chaplains; the Revd Francis Arthur Mann, Rector of St Margaret's, Walmgate, having taken over from the Revd E.C. Smith in 1921, was, in turn, replaced by the Revd Edward Etheringham Milner, Rector of St Mary, Castlegate, from 1929 to 1935 when the Revd Reginald Trevor Hughes, Rector of St Margaret's, Walmgate was appointed at the same salary of £100 that a predecessor had had 60 years earlier, a period in which the number of burials had only fallen from 1,212 to 1,019 in the financial year and the chaplain's share from 674 to 244.[23]

The Superintendent, Harry Robertson, retired in 1937 having worked for the company for 29 years, a period in which his salary had risen from £120 to £500 a year. He was then living at 25 Kilburn Road, part of the Kilburn estate that had belonged to the Agar family. His new house, built for him by the cemetery company in 1935, had cost £955 11s 4d, and his widow continued to live there until her death in 1954. The new superintendent was W. Bowyer but he resigned in November 1937 to be replaced by Robert William Boulton, the man who was to see the cemetery company through to its end. He was a professional gardener who had joined the company in 1925 and had risen by 1937 to be Robertson's assistant.[24]

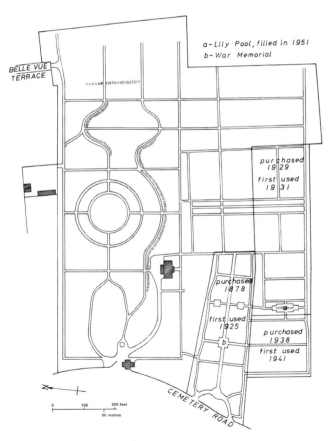

Plan 6 – York Cemetery 1910–Present

In February 1938, shortly after Boulton's appointment, the company made its last purchase of land. The York Conservative Club was paid £500 for a one acre field which it had bought from the Agar estate in 1929 and had since been used as a sports field. It was approved as a burial ground by the Minister of Health in 1940 despite a legal opinion from Ernest Wetton of the Temple (Wilfrid Gutch had retired) that approval was not necessary as the company were not operating under any of the Burial Acts. He also confirmed Gutch's opinion of 1912 that none of the occupants of houses that had been built within 100 yards had any right to object to burials in it other than for common nuisance. It was consecrated by the Bishop of Selby, the Rt Revd Carey Frederick Knyvett, on 15 May 1941 and the first burial was made in what was to be known as the 'football pitch' on 13 August. The York Public Cemetery Company had extended its land to just over 24¼ acres and its useful life by a few years but a decision still had to be taken on its future.[25]

The solution was to extend the monumental business, not only in the stone-yard at York Cemetery, which was already doing outside work, but by the purchase of others in towns elsewhere in Yorkshire, when the opportunity arose. The first to be acquired was Driffield Memorial Company. Negotiations with the owner, A. J. Pape, started early in 1940 and eventually his business and stock were purchased for £1,655. It made its first contribution to the profits of the company on 25 June 1941 with a modest sum, £99 7s 4d, which was improved on considerably thereafter (figure v). The interment account, while showing a small profit at the beginning of the Second World War, was nevertheless still a cause for concern. Burial numbers were gradually falling, the halcyon days of the company having almost a complete monopoly for the disposal of the dead in York were gone and would never return. Improvements in public health, an alternative method of disposal and competition from other cemeteries were all taking their toll on the burial business of the York Public Cemetery Company which, by the end of the war, was running at a loss which was showing every sign of getting larger.[26]

Figure v	Interment Account Profit/Loss	York Stone-yard Profit/Loss	Driffield Stone-yard Profit/Loss	Combined Profit Int. & St-yd.	Number of Burials	Dividend
	£ s d	£ s d	£ s d	£ s d		
1936	+1029 7 9	+2396 3 6		+3425 11 3	895*	10%+ £1
1937	+1404 6 7	+3038 15 4		+4443 1 11	1019*	10%+ £1
1938	+ 291 15 6	+3417 16 8		+3709 12 2	885*	10%+ £1
1939	+ 104 0 3	+3017 1 5		+3121 1 8	868*	10%+ £1
1940	+ 811 16 8	+2982 10 3		+3794 6 11	1100*	10%+15%
1941	+ 266 5 1	+3104 7 2	+ 99 4 7	+3469 16 10	921*	10%+15%
1942	+ 686 12 4	+2278 12 6	+439 9 1	+3404 13 11	918*	10%+15%
1943	+ 777 15 11	+2578 2 10	+379 18 0	+3735 16 9	938§	10%+15%
1944	+ 345 1 1	+3604 11 0	+463 2 0	+4412 14 1	855§	10%+15%
1945	- 422 0 8	+3840 7 2	+293 0 7	+3711 7 1	821§	10%+15%
1946	- 688 11 7	+3861 10 7	+736 7 11	+3909 6 11	703*	10%+15%

* calendar year   § financial year

York Cemetery was the recipient of one of the first four bombs to fall on York in the Second World War. It fell on 11 August 1940 in the Lawn Park Section, clear of any graves, making a crater 12 feet wide and six feet deep.

Before the Second World War was a year old the cemetery received a place in the record books that it can hardly have hoped to achieve. On 11 August 1940 it was the recipient of the first German bomb dropped on York. This was a high explosive bomb which fell in the Lawn Park Section on soft ground adjacent to a tarmac path and 10 yards from the nearest grave leaving a crater 12 feet wide and six feet deep. Much superficial damage was caused to nearby houses and gravestones. The Imperial War Grave Commission's Cross of Sacrifice was badly shaken. The pedestal block was moved ¼ inch from its setting, the shaft was fractured three feet up from the pedestal and much damage was done to the stonework by flying shrapnel; wilful damage certainly but the cemetery company could not have taken any 'reasonable precautions' to prevent it happening.

York was again a centre of military activity during the Second World War, with two Command Headquarters within its boundaries and surrounded by many army camps and Royal Air Force stations. The majority of graves of service casualties from this war, 190, are at Fulford but there are 85 in York Cemetery, six sailors, 55 soldiers, 23 airmen and one member of the Air Training Corps, Cadet

William Anthony Lain, who died on 26 July 1946 aged 17. While the ATC was a civilian organisation, it was recognised that its members' graves ranked for war graves. Since 1948 the Commission has erected 64 of its standard headstones on these graves. Of the 31 graves with privately provided memorials, 11 have a Commission headstone as well. After the war, in 1949, the Commission provided a new cross in Portland stone, an exact replica of the original, to be a central memorial to the servicemen of both world wars. The replacement does not have a legend on its base as it was not the general policy of the Imperial (Commonwealth since 1960) War Graves Commission to put inscriptions on Second World War crosses.[27]

The blast of the bomb moved the Cross of Sacrifice a quarter of an inch out of alignment and fractured its shaft. It was replaced by a replica in 1949.

[Photograph courtesy of the Commonwealth War Graves Commission]

The Revd Trevor Hughes resigned as cemetery chaplain in 1941 and was succeeded by the Revd Charles Ernest Emerson, Rector of St Margaret's, Walmgate, who held the post until 1952. Next was the Revd David Parry Bodycombe, Rector of St Chad's, who was followed in 1954 by the Revd Edward Broughton Parr Duckworth, Rector of St Clement's. Then in 1956 came the Revd William Pickering, Vicar of Fulford who asked, in 1960, for his fees to be raised but, after hearing from Robert Boulton that in the last two years the chaplain had only officiated at an average of 70 interments each year, his application was refused by the cemetery committee. Pickering was replaced in 1964 by the Revd Alfred Richard Jones, Rector of St Lawrence's, who held the office for the final years of the cemetery company.

In 1944 the two surviving trustees, William Seale and James Frederick Bushell, were joined by Raymond Edward Warner, Wine Merchant, and Charles Wilfrid Robinson, Company Director, and these four presided over the last days of the York Public Cemetery Company.[28] Once the war was over they took a step suggested by Harry Robertson in 1929 and discussed at great length ever since then. On 19 October 1945 the four trustees became the first directors of the York Cemetery Company Ltd., No. 399607 on the register of companies, which had a share capital of £6,000 divided into 600 shares of £10 each. It still operated under the terms of the Deed of Settlement of 1838 but these had, with the passage of time, become obsolete or inappropriate. The Companies Act contained a model form of articles for public companies and this formed the basis of the Memorandum and Articles of Association which were adopted at an extraordinary general meeting held at 24 Pavement, the office of the company's secretaries, the solicitors Teasdale, Hewitt and Holden, held on 14 August 1954.

The directors at this time were:

Charles Wilfrid Robinson, Chairman, J.J. Hunt Ltd, Brewers
Robert Brocket Holden, Solicitor
Arthur Raney, Schoolmaster
George Woollons, Hardware Dealer
George Bernard Woollons, Hardware Dealer
Robert William Boulton, Cemetery Superintendent

Besides listing the normal procedures for operating a company and defining its core business as managing the cemetery and supplying monumental masonry the Memorandum of Association gave them wide ranging objectives in a variety of associated and other fields. It could maintain cemeteries in other localities, carry on business as funeral directors and undertakers, build and operate crematoria and supply wreathes of all types. Other activities allowed were purchasing and managing estates and property, manufacturing and dealing in granite, stone, cement, artificial stone, brick, tile, pottery, earthenware and china, owning quarries, trading as nurserymen, horticulturists, market gardeners and printers and, finally, in a catch-all clause, carrying on: -

any other businesses whatsoever which may seem to the company capable of being conveniently carried on in connection with the above objects or any of them or calculated directly or indirectly to enhance the value of or render more profitable any of the company's property.

Harry Robertson would have been delighted to know that the company could now establish and maintain any contributory or non-contributory pension or superannuation for the benefit of the directors and employees![29]

Less than 18 months after the formation of the new company, Robert Boulton, the superintendent, at a monthly meeting of the cemetery committee expressed some doubts about the future. The result was that a works committee was set up to 'suggest some policy which may correct any unhappy feature and .... tend to further exploit the successful activities of the company for the benefit of all concerned'. In setting out its findings in 'as few sentences as possible' the committee had 'neither praise nor blame in mind'. It simply tried 'to put on paper the salient facts of the present position of the company and also what may be the possibilities for the future'. The committee's approach to its task was to compare the results of the most recent financial year, 1946 (see figure v), with the average of the last five stable pre-war years, 1934-1938. In this 'standard year', when there had been 922 burials, the stone-yard had shown a profit of £2,743 and the cemetery £949.

The monumental business of the stone-yard, now supplemented by the Driffield Memorial Company, had continued to be very satisfactory but the ratio of profit to sales had fallen from 45% in the standard year to 33% in 1946. It was thought that this would fall further due to increased competition now that the war was over, the transference of some costs, for policy reasons, from the stone-yard to the cemetery and the adverse effect of the opening of a municipal cemetery which York Corporation was then planning. On the other hand the cemetery account showed a continued and increasing debit balance caused by a heavy decrease in the number of interments and a large increase in the costs of working the cemetery. It would be possible to raise extra income by raising the fees, but they had already been increased fairly recently to a level above those of the company's competitors, or by offering commissions to undertakers as a means of securing more interments, an idea which was rejected because of its possible illegality. Working costs, on the other hand, could be reduced by strict economy and supervision and by employing less staff. In the standard year there had been nine employees, working a 48 hour week, dealing with 102.4 interments per man while in 1946 ten, on a 45½ hour week, had only dealt with 70.3 each. While the addition of one acre to the cemetery in 1938 had increased the work connected with the care of graves to a small extent it appeared that the cemetery was over staffed.

The works committee concluded its report with a pat on the back for the company. 'It would therefore appear that, with our widespread reputation, and with our facilities for business well organised, we may with confidence anticipate many years of successful trading.' With wise management it was expected that the company would be able to provide a dividend for many years to come especially as, with falling consumption, there were sufficient grave spaces for the next 15 years. While considerable progress had been made before the war for the conversion of the company into two separate businesses, monumental and cemetery, this was now thought to be an impracticable change, even if advisable. A cloud on the horizon was the possible nationalisation of commercial cemetery companies which was then being openly advocated in the House of Commons.[30]

Despite the only positive suggestion in the report for reducing expenditure the number of staff employed in the cemetery stayed at much the same level, varying between nine and twelve for most of the remainder of the life of York Cemetery Company. Not until 1965, when there were only six, was there any substantial reduction. The losses continued to increase except for the three years after 1958 when the effects of the introduction of a new scale of fees temporarily reversed the trend, something which further revisions in 1963 and 1965 failed to do. All efforts were seemingly concentrated on improving the memorial business which had been affected by the public fashion in ordering smaller and less expensive headstones and the restrictions placed on memorials in corporation owned cemeteries. By 1953 a Mr Tasker at Goole was acting as an agent for the company and making memorials at his premises there. In the same year a policy of outright acquisition of stone-yards was begun when the business being run by Edgar Beven in Union Lane, Selby was bought together with the adjoining house, 1 Portholme Villas, for £2,452 14s 7d. A much smaller sum, £100, in 1954 secured from Warner Brothers the remainder of their interest in the lease of a yard of 400 square yards in Castleford together with a brick-built workshop and shed. Finally Scarborough Memorial Company was purchased in 1962 but this did not live up to expectations and was disposed of by the beginning of 1966.[31]

The company did not want to limit itself to monumental masonry. In 1956, in accordance with the powers given it by the Memorandum of Association, the superintendent was asked to circularise architects and builders who might be interested in placing stone masonry work with the company. Six months later the fact that it was prepared to carry out stone masonry, carving and the restoration of buildings and monuments was advertised to all and sundry. This does not appear to have had any significant effect but by 1960 there had been a substantial increase in the sale of memorials and Robert Boulton was instructed to increase the company's sales area and even to consider the appointment of another representative to exploit the new area. A new approach in 1962 was the suggested entry into the wholesale market but by this time the company was in its terminal stages and this was not pursued but enquiries were made in 1963 to see if selling memorials on hire purchase might stimulate extra business.[32]

Another problem to occupy the minds of the directors was an attempt to raise the rateable value of the cemetery which, had it been successful, would have further diminished the hard won overall profitability of the company. In April 1956 it was told that the rateable value was to be increased from £585 to £1,750. The superintendent was asked to find a valuer who specialised in cemetery rating and the company wrote to the cemetery companies at Bradford and Sheffield to see if their rates had been increased. When their replies were received, presumably saying that they had not had an increase in their rates or at least such a Draconian increase, the York Cemetery Company decided in July 1957 to appeal against the new valuation. A year later a representative of York Corporation offered to reduce the valuation to £750 but after some negotiation a final figure of £675 was reached by October 1957 and agreed by the company in July 1958.[33]

Despite all these vicissitudes in the fortunes of the company its shareholders can have had nothing to complain about. In 1951 the 30% dividend which had been paid for some years was increased to 50% and maintained at that level until 1962 (figure vi). There were, of course, other sources of revenue that helped to sustain this high level of dividend payment, particularly the interest on the fairly substantial investments which the company had in stocks and shares. These had been listed in the balance sheet in 1947 at a cost price of £22,759. As the equivalent figure in 1964 was £22,443 it was obvious that the only real changes that had been made to the portfolio had been to pay a dividend in 1963. Some dated stocks had been redeemed and the proceeds reinvested but no new purchases had been made to increase the holdings for 17 years. All or nearly all of the yearly profits had been paid to the shareholders to maintain their customary 50% dividend. The dividend was reduced in 1963 to 12% (£720) paid out of capital, a step decided upon after seeking an opinion from Christopher Slade of Lincoln's Inn on its legality. His enquiries revealed that the capital mostly represented past profits and that, while the Grave Planting Fund was not large enough for the company to fulfil the contractual obligations it had entered into with some 80 grave owners to maintain their graves in perpetuity, some capital could be used for a dividend. If the directors had recommended the payment of a dividend out of capital without ensuring there were sufficient reserves to meet commitments it could be argued that it was paid in fraud and they would be liable to repay it out of their own pockets if ever the company was wound up.[34]

Figure vi	Interment Account Profit/Loss £	Stone yards Profit/Loss £	Combined Profit Int. & Styds £	Number of Burials	Dividend
1952	-1102	+2502	+1400	610	50%
1953	-151	+4776	+4625	614	50%
1954	-237	+3485	+3248	643	50%
1955	-938	+3884	+2946	614	50%
1956	-2821	+6830	+4009	558	50%
1957	-1196	+2689	+1493	469	50%
1958	-1684	+3897	+2213	493	50%
1959	+310	+2205	+2515	382	50%
1960	+1314	+1118	+2432	409	50%
1961	-932	+6766	+5834	409	50%
1962	-2773	+6447	+3674	344	50%
1963	-2127	+4208	+2081	339	12%
1964	-2443	+3869	+1426	258	0%
1965	-1456	+4950	+3494	268	0%

This was followed by no dividend payment at all in 1964, a recognition that the life of the company was limited. C.W. Robinson, in explaining this unpalatable news to the shareholders in 1964, said that the burden of maintaining the cemetery was an ever-increasing one. All prudent economies had been exercised and about £500 had been saved by cutting director's fees, increasing some fees and leaving the greenhouse unheated, but the loss had increased. The profit on the memorial account was reduced and after the manager's salary and the director's fees had been paid as well as some legal and accountancy charges the company had sustained a loss of £45. No dividend could be paid

> and in spite of the considerable resources of the Company, it could not continue to fulfil its obligations to the public by keeping the cemetery in good order, and your Directors feel they must make approach to the Local Authority with a view to being relieved of this responsibility.

The shareholders were, however, promised that they would be given the opportunity of approving any agreement reached.[35]

When the cemetery company, in 1931, laid out the strip of land which it had purchased from Joseph Agar, a trustee who lived at Kilburn House on the southern boundary, it continued the park theme by including a Lily Pool at its west end. The pool was filled in in 1951 to provide more burial space.

[Photograph courtesy of Mrs. Alma Winship]

In addition to the cost of maintaining the cemetery there were, apparently, now no burial spaces left for sale so no further revenue could be gained from this source. The last purchase of land had been made in 1938 and there was no more available adjacent to the cemetery. To maximise the use of what remained to them the directors had, in 1952, decided to remove the cupressus trees lining the main avenue to make more room. Nevertheless in 1954 it was reported that there were only 200 grave spaces left, 19 in 1960 and none at all in 1963. This is an inexplicable situation. The York Cemetery Trust, since becoming the owner of the cemetery, has positively identified 450 unused grave spaces and there are certainly many more. It may, however, have been a tactical move to expedite the process of winding up the company. In 1962, the previous year, on the basis of the facts made known to them by the cemetery management the York Branch of the National Association of Funeral Directors foresaw difficulties. Any person wishing to be buried rather than cremated would have to be taken outside the city boundary, to Fulford or elsewhere, to the discomfiture of the relatives.

Robert Boulton told them that family graves in York cemetery could, of course, be opened if there was still room in them but it was now up to the Corporation – `they have known for years that there would be a shortage of burial space'.[36]

The cemetery company, intent on maximising the profitability of the stone-yard was accused in 1963 of operating a closed shop policy. `Mourners', said the *Yorkshire Evening Press*, `can take tombstones through the gates to the cemetery. But to do so they must pay up to £40 for the privilege'. The fee charged for memorials made by an outside mason depended on its shape and size – a monumental vase was a mere £3 unless it had an epitaph when a few treasured words would double the fee to £6 6s. For a monument made by the cemetery company, however, there was no extra charge. This had been the practice for a long time and the local masons had been upset for many years. Robert Boulton retorted that a private company was quite entitled to do this; there could be big business in burials and it was not sharp practice. The company had to pay rates of £700 a year as well as the wages of the staff to keep the cemetery tidy. In 126 years it had not been subsidised by the Corporation but, with no more room for new graves, there was a possibility that in the near future York Corporation and the City's ratepayers would find it to be their duty to take over and maintain this private cemetery – a portent of things to come.[37]

Christopher Slade had also been asked for his opinion in 1963 on what steps the company could take to reduce or eliminate its liability to maintain the cemetery. He thought the most promising line of approach, as far as the individual shareholders were concerned, was to negotiate a sale of their shares to York Corporation. The cemetery was practically full and was in a reasonable state. The revenue from the sale of memorials was expected to diminish very rapidly and it would therefore become increasingly difficult for the company to maintain the cemetery which would get into a worse and worse state. Sooner or later the company would be forced into liquidation and then York Corporation, however unwilling, may be forced to take over the management and upkeep of the cemetery in the absence of any other person or body able and willing to do so. It would be better, Slade argued, for the Corporation to buy the shares and take over the running of the cemetery while it was still reasonably prosperous, in good order and possessing substantial assets rather than be forced, reluctantly, to take over a derelict concern with all its assets dissipated in the course of liquidation as had happened in the case of the Nottingham cemetery. The company's solicitors, however, thought that there were several difficulties in following this line. The Corporation would not want the memorial business and the shareholders would not be likely to agree a price for their shares that the Corporation could afford as the company possessed considerable assets at this time. The directors thought their best plan would be to carry on and even expand the memorials business. Dividends could be paid until there were only sufficient funds left to maintain their obligations to grave owners. When this stage was reached the cemetery could be disposed of to York Corporation on nominal terms.[38]

Before any negotiations could be started with the Corporation an approach was made in November 1963 by G.A. Kaye Ltd., wood-carvers in the Shambles, who suggested that the two companies should be amalgamated. This firm was asked to make specific proposals in writing but nothing more was heard from it. The Corporation, in line with the advice given by Counsel, was informed in October 1964 that the directors wished to ask if it would relieve the company of its responsibilities now when it still had some resources rather than wait until they were exhausted and the cemetery was derelict. The terms suggested were that the freehold of the cemetery and all its buildings, the vehicles and equipment used in operating the cemetery and the company's investments were transferred to the Corporation in return for it undertaking responsibility for maintaining the cemetery and certain graves. The company wished to retain the use of the stone-yard and its buildings, the showroom and the office in the lodge at a rent to be agreed. The Corporation's reply was not encouraging. It thought that the assets would not produce sufficient income to pay the wages of the staff necessary to maintain the cemetery, the land value was nil and would be a liability and there was no legal obligation for it to acquire the cemetery. In the event the Corporation decided that neither was there any moral obligation to do so. The York Cemetery Company Ltd was now left with one course of action – voluntary liquidation.[39]

Once more Christopher Slade was asked for an opinion; could the company be wound up voluntarily and how should this be done? His reply on 26 March 1965 said that it would be first necessary for the directors to make a Declaration of Solvency stating that the company would be able to pay its debts in full within twelve months of the liquidation procedure commencing and then a special resolution should be passed to give authority to the decision to wind up the company. The liabilities of the company to those persons with whom it had entered into a contractual obligation to maintain particular graves, the agreement to keep the lawn graves clipped, rolled and planted with grass without charge and the liability to keep available for use those grave spaces for which burial rights still existed should be considered before the Declaration of Solvency was made. An honest and careful attempt should be made by the directors to assess the financial damage which would be suffered by the interested parties if these obligations were not carried out. Only after considering these matters in great detail should the directors make the required declaration which would have the advantage that the winding up would be in the hands of the members of the company rather than its creditors.[40]

The cemetery committee considered this reply at their meetings on 14 April, 26 July and 6 October when the question of liquidation was postponed to 13 January 1966 when a final decision would be made. The decision at that meeting was that an extraordinary meeting would be held on 31 March when the motion to be put was 'that the company be wound up by the Court and that its directors be authorised and directed to present a petition to the Court on its behalf and in its name and to take all steps necessary for that purpose.' A statement from the chairman was to be sent to all shareholders setting out alternative proposals. When the day for the extraordinary meeting arrived there were only four people present, G. Woollons, G.B. Woollens, A. Raney and R.W. Boulton, and on a show of hands the proposal was carried unanimously. This formality over the directors then proceeded to hold the final committee meeting of York Cemetery Company Ltd at which the chairman expressed his appreciation of the loyal service to the company rendered by R.W. Boulton and other members of the company's staff over the years. Boulton, on telling the cemetery committee that he would have to seek other employment, had had his salary raised by £500 to £1,525 a year on 29 July 1965, back-dated to 1 July 1964, and he would be 65 years old in September 1966 when he would have retired in any case but the loyalty of the rest of the staff was to be rewarded by the immediate prospect of enforced redundancy.[41]

NOTES

1. YCA Acc. 107/38; *Yorkshire Gazette* 15 May 1909; Kelly's *Directory of York* (1914) p 9.
2. YCA Acc. 247/102.
3. YCM 1909/10 pp 1341; *York Cemetery and Company Fees Regulations* (1912) p 2.
4. *Suggestions to Burial Boards providing and managing Burial Grounds, and making Arrangements for Interments under the Burial Acts of 1852-3-4-5 and 7.*
5. YCA Acc 247/105 Annual Reports 1920, 1921, 1922 and 1923.
6. *The War Graves of the British Empire* Yorkshire 9-98, Cemeteries within the East Riding of Yorkshire and the City and County Borough of York (1929) pp 15-20, 30-37.
7. E.M. Smith, MOH, *Report on Influenza and the Influenza Epidemic of 1918*, 13 February 1919; Yorkshire Herald 27 July 1918 and 31 October 1918.

8. YCA Acc. 247/98.
9. YCA Acc. 247/107a.
10. York Public Cemetery Company *Rules and Regulations* (1932) p 3.
11. R.A. Fellows *An Edwardian Architect* (1985); *Yorkshire Gazette* 30 May 1925.
12. YCA Acc. 247/110.
13. YCA 247/118.
14. YCA Acc. 247/118a, /118d, /120.
15. YCA BC19/9 pp 153 & 172; YCA BB52/2 pp 98, 113, 119.
16. Friends of York Cemetery Archive, Miscellaneous Letters 50.
17. YCA Acc. 247/121.
18. YCA Acc. 247/144.
19. YCA Acc. 247/120.
20. YCM 1931/32 pp 346 & 524.
21. York Public Cemetery Company *Rules and Regulations* (1932) p5; YCA Acc. 247/155 Annual Reports 1935/6 & 1936/7.
22. YCA Acc. 247/126.
23. YCA Acc. 247/155 Annual Reports 1935/6, 1936/7 and 1937/8.
24. YCA Acc. 247/155 Annual Report 1937/8; Yorkshire Evening Press 31 December 1986.
25. YCA Acc. 247/128; YCA Acc. 247/134.
26. YCA Acc. 247/155 Annual Reports 1939/40 to 1945/6.
27. *1939-1945 The War Dead of the Commonwealth Cemeteries and Churchyards in Yorkshire, II* (1961) pp 31-38, VII (1962) pp 4044; Letter from Commonwealth War Grave Commission to York Cemetery Trust, 10 January 1990.
28. YCA Acc. 247/135.
29. *Memorandum and Articles of Association of York Cemetery Company Ltd.* (1953).
30. YCA Acc. 247/136.
31. YCA Acc. 239 Add., Committee Minute Book No. 9, 7 April 1953, 25 February 1954, 2 April 1962, 7 Jan 1965.
32. YCA Acc. 239 Add., Committee Minute Book No. 9, 4 October 1956, 10 April 1957, 18 July 1960, 4 Jan 1962, 3 October 1963.
33. YCA Acc. 239 Add., Committee Minute Book No. 9, 12 April, 23 May, 16 July 1956, 19 August, 3 October 1957, 17 July 1958.
34. YCA Acc. 247/155 Annual Report 1963/4; YCA Acc. 247/145c.
35. YCA Acc. 239 Add., Committee Minute Book No. 9, 8 August 1963; YCA Acc. 247/145; YCA Acc. 247/155 Annual Report 1963/4.
36. YCA Acc. 239 Add., Committee Minute Book No. 9, 2 October 1952, 12 April 1960; YCA Acc. 247/145; Yorkshire Evening Press 24 February 1962.
37. *Yorkshire Evening Press* 7 December 1963.
38. YCA Acc. 247/144a, /145b.
39. YCA Acc. 239 Add., Committee Minute Book No. 9, 13 November 1963, 9 January 1964, 16 October 1964, 7 January 1965.
40. YCA Acc. 247/147.
41. YCA Acc. 239 Add., Committee Minute Book No. 9, 14 April, 29 July, 6 October 1965, 13 January, 31 March 1966.

6: 'Not Born for Death'- Rebirth and Revival

Thou wast not born for death, immortal bird! No hungry generations tread thee down

J. Keats Ode to a Nightingale

With the decision to wind up the company made, the directors lost no time in starting the necessary procedures. On 9 May 1966 a petition was presented to the High Court of Justice, Chancery Division, Companies Court which made a winding up order on 13 June on the application of the Official Receiver who had examined the obligations of the York Cemetery Company and had found a decline in profitability of its operations since 1961. This same official became the provisional liquidator and two days later appointed Ian Anthony Scott, a York solicitor, as special manager of the estate and business of the company. In similar circumstances most companies ceased trading but as this was not possible for a public cemetery the liquidator decided that business should continue as before.[1] A solicitor had been chosen for this task because of the complex legal problems that were associated with the winding up of a cemetery.

But even before he was officially appointed Scott had begun his task and had visited the cemetery on 14 June 1966 where he met the superintendent, R.W. Boulton, and was given details of the company. He was told that the stonework department made and maintained memorials both for York cemetery, other cemeteries and private customers. There were five employees, three at York, one who lived at and managed the company's business at Driffield and another living at Selby, responsible for the stone-yards there and at Castleford. There was no work in progress at York as the employees were out delivering completed orders but new memorial work worth between £3000 and £5000 had yet to be started. The stonework department was definitely profitable but had had to cover the cemetery losses. Apart from wages of about £120 a week its expenses were small, just the cost of electricity, water rates and transport. The first amounted to some £60 a year and petrol costs were about £12 a week for the fleet of five vehicles. Boulton further estimated that the value of the whole business at York and elsewhere was about £7,000 for premises, £4,500 for stock and £1,750 for goodwill.

In the cemetery there were two gardeners whose principal work was the maintenance of graves. There were approximately 570 annual contracts, varying between £1 10s 0d to £2 12s 6d each, for keeping graves tidy and planted, and some 57 agreements to maintain graves, either in perpetuity or for the life of the cemetery, for which sums between £10 and £250 had been paid. Additionally one of the gardeners cleaned the office and the public toilets. Three grave-diggers were also employed and they and the gardeners assisted each other as required. The wage bill amounted to about £64 a week but the other expenses of running the cemetery depended on the number of burials and the use of the chapel. The reason that the company had applied to be wound up was that the land resources of the cemetery were almost exhausted. Boulton said there was no easy way of calculating the room that remained in existing graves or the number of grave spaces still available, a statement somewhat at variance with his earlier declaration that there were none. He was fully responsible for running the company, assisted by a clerk earning £8 10s 0d a week, only meeting the chairman and other directors formally at quarterly board meetings and informally when he needed cheques signing.[2]

A statutory meeting of creditors was held on 8 July following which the Court, on 22 July, appointed Scott as liquidator of the York Cemetery Company, reporting to a committee of inspection. Boulton continued to run the cemetery on a day to day basis until his retirement on 30 September when Walter Grayson, who had worked in the cemetery as a gardener since 15 November 1952, took over the responsibility for supervising three grave-diggers, identifying grave spaces, liaising with the stone-yard for the removal and replacement of memorials and carrying out the contractual obligations for grave maintenance.[3] From this list of duties it can be seen that some men in both the stone-yard and the cemetery, as well as the office clerk, had been re-employed when their notice had expired on 13 June 1966.

Two courses of action were open to Scott. The first was to go to court and disclaim further responsibility for the cemetery and the contractual obligations the company had made for grave maintenance and the continuity of burial in family graves which, it was said, had sufficient space in them for at least 15,000 bodies. Alternatively he could try to get another party to take over the complete organisation. Although he was already running the cemetery he could not continue this task indefinitely as his duty as a liquidator was to administer the affairs of the company only until the liquidation was complete. The obvious choice as the new owner was York Corporation who had already turned down an offer from the company in 1964 but, nevertheless, Scott made an informal approach to enquire if its position had changed. Under the Open Spaces Act 1906 a local authority could have a disused burial ground conveyed to it by its owner to use as a place of public recreation – not for organised games and sports but as a park in which the public could walk and sit while still preserving the peaceful atmosphere of its original use.

If this were to happen the Corporation could clear away all the headstones and memorials and lay out the site with paths, lawns and flowers beds, a possibility which concerned the Commonwealth War Graves Commission who had, and still have, the responsibility for the care and maintenance of the 234 war graves in York cemetery. It was opposed to any disturbance of remains unless there was no practical alternative and if the individual Commission headstones were removed it would want some alternative memorial provided at the expense of the new owners, possibly a screen wall, surrounding the Cross of Sacrifice, on which the names of the war dead could be engraved. Its preferred alternative, however, was for the cemetery to continue in use. The Corporation, no doubt, was reluctant to use the powers given it by the Open Spaces Act 1906 as it could then become liable to pay compensation for extinguishing the 57 perpetual grave maintenance contracts and the rights of an unspecified number of owners of burial rights. A better course of action would be to let the liquidator disclaim the cemetery and all its obligations and then reconsider its position.

While discussions were in progress Scott was looking after the interests of the 71 shareholders, who owned between them the 600 shares in York Cemetery Company, by disposing of various assets not directly connected with the cemetery. By January 1967 he had sold the cemetery superintendent's house, 25 Kilburn Road, as well as the stone-yards at Driffield and Selby. This, after settling with creditors, increased the company's surpluses, which at the time the liquidation commenced had been estimated to exceed £29,000. From this the costs of continuing to run the cemetery would have had to have been met but, by April 1967, these had been reduced to a minimum by closing the stone-yard, the once profitable jewel in the cemetery's crown, and only retaining a skeleton staff of five men to deal with burials and the maintenance agreements.[4]

The chapel in May 1969, shortly after the Cemetery Company started the liquidation proceedings, shows little sign that it was soon to he considered unsafe. At this time the central path is still lined with carefully trimmed hedges.

[Photograph courtesy of the Royal Commission on Historical Monuments, England]

These cost cutting measures brought many grumbles and complaints about the apparent neglect of the cemetery. Mr Brian Rowan, who made a weekly visit to his mother's grave thought the state of the graveyard disgusting, the worst cemetery in the country. He had been unable to locate his grandfather's grave in a wilderness of tall grass. In some areas, where there were what Scott called lawn graves, the grass was clipped but a controversy arose here when Alan Buck was ordered to remove a few flowers which his wife had planted round his father's grave 'in direct contravention of the cemetery company's rules'. This was rubbing salt into a wound opened the previous year when he had had to pay five guineas for the privilege of putting a black marble vase on the grave. He was not going to remove the flowers and if the cemetery staff did he would sue them for stealing. Scott explained that kerbs, mounds, glass and artificial ornaments were forbidden in the lawn areas by the regulations and nobody could be permitted to put flowers round graves. All these additions to a grave would make maintenance more difficult and more costly.[5]

With little or no progress being made in negotiations with the Corporation Scott started formal proceedings on 19 July 1967 with an application to the court to disclaim the cemetery, all implied contracts with the holders of grave certificates and with all other persons entitled to rights of burial and all contracts for the upkeep of graves. The first hearing of the summons, scheduled for 31 July, was adjourned until 17 October to allow notice to be given to all interested persons by the means of advertisements placed in newspapers.[6] At the same time the shareholders of the cemetery company, the Crown Estate Commissioners, York Corporation and the Commonwealth War Graves Commission were formally informed of the application. The last hearing of the summons was on 16 January 1968 when it was once again adjourned for a date to be fixed, a formula which would allow time for an amicable agreement to be reached with York Corporation for it to take over the cemetery after settlement with all creditors. This delay also gave the various interested parties an opportunity to make their cases in opposition to the liquidator's intentions.

The Commonwealth Wars Graves Commission wished to ensure that its graves were maintained in a dignified and suitable setting which could only be achieved if there was not a period when nobody was responsible for the cemetery. The holders of burial rights would suffer financial loss not only in losing their already purchased plots but further by having to buy a space elsewhere. Even if they were given some financial compensation for this nothing could replace their wish and their right to be buried with their relatives. The loss to persons with maintenance contracts was more difficult to quantify. The tidy state of their graves was obviously important to them but possibly this could be ensured if some of the funds of the cemetery company were used to remove kerbstones and to set up a long term maintenance contract. The Corporation had a duty to prevent an abandoned cemetery becoming a statutory nuisance, which it thought would be inevitable, and possibly a health hazard if further burials were made with no one in control of the cemetery. If the disclaimer were allowed and the Crown Estates Commissioners, who were keeping a low profile and not revealing their intentions, did not take possession of the land the Corporation would find itself in the position of having to make expenditure, a burden on the ratepayers, to keep the cemetery in reasonable condition. There were large surpluses in the cemetery's accounts which would be distributed to the shareholders if the liquidator's plan was successful. It would be better if these were used to maintain the cemetery rather than allow them to benefit shareholders who, over the years, had already had a considerable return on their investment.

Over the years an accumulation of greenhouses, seen here in 1972, were built at the south end of the gatehouse. Provided for the cultivation of plants for the cemetery, the first was built before 1891.

With the Court hearing adjourned the process of trying to find a solution to the cemetery's problems settled down to a long period of apparent inactivity, with little prospect of reconciling the disparate interests of the two parties. The Corporation, if it was to take over the financial incubus that the cemetery would represent, would have wanted all its assets and reserves to offset the burden on the ratepayers. This would appear, at first sight, to be a reasonable attitude as it could be said that the shareholders had enjoyed, for many years, considerable dividend payments but, at the same time, the company had built up large reserves giving lie to the often stated calumny that it was their milking of the company which had brought about the liquidation. The liquidator, on the other hand, who had been appointed to represent the shareholders, would have wanted to wind up the company with the maximum return for them, the cemetery abandoned and all its realisable assets distributed in proportion to their individual shareholdings. At the very least he would surely have wanted to retain £6,000 for them, the face value of the shares, still leaving over £23,000 for the Corporation.

In the meantime Scott continued to run the cemetery with his skeleton staff. The number of burials (140 in 1967, 161 in 1968, 192 in 1969) was sufficient to allow him to cover all costs with stringent management. In 1968 he raised the burial fees then, on 1 March 1969, he introduced a number of measures designed to save unnecessary expenditure. While people wanting grave certificate or grave number details would not be charged others, presumably genealogists and family historians, in view of the time and effort expended in tracing the relevant entries, would be charged a search fee of 10s 0d. No at-cost price public burials had been made for some time so this facility was withdrawn and the already opened public graves were filled in. If cemetery staff were to dig the grave undertakers were required to give at least 48 hours notice of an intended interment, having first removed all masonry and memorials from the grave. After any burial the stonework was to be replaced by the undertakers not later than nine months after the opening of the grave. If this was not done defaulting undertakers would not be allowed to open further graves until they had complied with this requirement. In any case they would be held responsible for any damage or loss caused by loose memorials lying around.[7] Apart from this problem memorials were becoming an increasing worry for Scott. The ravages of time on their fixings, exacerbated by the ravages of recent gales, caused many of them to lean over at dangerous angles. They were liable to collapse which could possibly injure visitors to the cemetery and children climbing over the walls to enter the cemetery when it was closed.[8]

But even if the directors of York Cemetery Company had decided that they could no longer run their business for the benefit of the shareholders there were others who thought that the cemetery could still be a viable undertaking. An undertaker from Easingwold wanted to buy the lodge, greenhouses, the stone-yard and the monumental masonry showroom as an extension to his already established business outside York and, in addition, was willing, if his offer to purchase these cemetery buildings was successful, to consider taking on a part-time employee as Cemetery Superintendent. From the liquidator's point of view a more attractive proposal was made by a York businessman who felt that the cemetery could still be of considerable benefit to the City and, with careful management, could produce an excess of income over expenditure for many years to come. He was prepared to offer £20 a share for all the assets and liabilities of the company if the disclaimer action was withdrawn. Without the burden of having to pay an annual dividend to the shareholders he thought that, even with hardly any space available for new graves, he would get an adequate return on his capital.[9]

The day-to-day difficulties of keeping the cemetery open continued to beset Scott. At the end of 1969 a passer-by in Cemetery Road had told him that some of the poplars which lined the boundary appeared to be diseased. An expert, who

At some time the appearance of the chapel, seen here in 1982, has been spoiled by the addition of sloping ramps on either side of the portico steps. These have been removed in the recent restoration.

[Photograph - Helen Kirk]

was called in to inspect them, advised him that they were dangerous and should be felled. Immediately this was done Edith Wilks, who lived at 60 Cemetery Road, wrote to the *Yorkshire Evening Press* complaining of this unnecessary vandalism, 'trees and shrubs in full beauty had been wantonly mowed down'. Scott's reply explaining that his decision was motivated purely for reasons of safety, was published alongside Edith Wilks' letter. In fact, hers was the only complaint, others had commended him for removing an unsightly mass of tangled undergrowth.[10] At the same time Scott had had to erect a fence around the chapel. This was necessary because, in the opinion of the Corporation's Chief Building Inspector, Henry Galpin, there was a real danger that its roof could collapse. Over the years water had penetrated the fabric at eaves level causing extensive settlement of the roof and ceiling. The local branch of the National Association of Funeral Directors, on being informed that this precaution would block the main drive, replied that they regretted the decay to such a fine and historic building and remarked, that its members were in no way responsible for its preservation, without any suggestion from Scott that they were, but the public should be warned by notices placed at a suitable distance from the building.[11]

The cemetery was now beginning to lose money. Undertakers were taking bodies to Fulford Parish cemetery, no doubt encouraged by the fact that this cemetery was better maintained than York Cemetery and the agreement York Corporation had made with Fulford Parish Council in 1969 which allowed York citizens to be buried there for the next 50 years for the same fee as parishioners rather than at the double charge made to people resident outside the parish. For this right the Corporation agreed to take responsibility for the losses in running Fulford cemetery in proportion to the number of York burials out of the total number.[12] The negotiations for the Corporation take-over after the completion of the disclaimer proceedings were still dragging slowly on, probably bogged down by the liquidator's insistence that the shareholders should receive some compensation. Many of the shareholders were beginning to ask when they could expect to receive any payment, so, perhaps to encourage the reaching of an agreement and at the same time, should this fail, to keep alive the interest of the businessman who wished to buy the cemetery, Scott made a survey of the cemetery and found, contrary to the stated position just before the liquidation had commenced, that there were up to 3000 new grave spaces in the cemetery and more could be made available by using some of the footpaths.[13]

Scott however had troubles of his own and, as a result of a Receiving Order in Bankruptcy made against him on 6 September 1971, he had to relinquish his post and hand over to the Official Receiver, who, on 8 September appointed George Eric Rushton, an accountant from Bradford, first as special manager and then on 23 November becoming the new liquidator. With the appointment of a new liquidator came a new enthusiasm to finish the task started, seemingly so long ago, in 1966. His first action was to decide not to renew any annual grave maintenance contracts after they elapsed at the end of 1971 and then, having grasped the state of play so far, Rushton reopened the hearing at the Companies Court. On 15 September 1972 he sought a ruling on which of two alternative courses he should follow – to disclaim the cemetery and then transfer it to the Corporation or abandon the proceedings and sell the cemetery as a going concern to the York businessman who had offered to buy it. He must have been disappointed with the Court's decision, more delay, and a postponement to allow more concrete proposals to be made.

If the cemetery company was wound up with all its contracts and obligations cancelled and the land and other assets transferred to the Corporation there would be no benefit for the shareholders, the holders of grave certificates would loose their burial rights and if, to reduce the maintenance costs, all memorials were removed and it was laid out as a park under the Open Spaces Act 1906, the Commonwealth War Graves Commission would insist that some of the cemetery's funds would have to be used to provide some other method of commemorating the war dead buried there. The alternative proposal would provide the shareholders with some recompense but it could possibly result in new liquidation proceedings starting at some time in the future when the private venture ceased to be profitable. Thus, caught on the horns of a dilemma, Rushton proceeded slowly on both fronts but his position was made easier in May 1973 when the businessman withdrew his offer leaving the field open to the Corporation.

While negotiations with the Corporation ground slowly on speculation and rumour abounded. Frank Buck, who had commemorated his father with an Italian marble monument sculpted with a replica of an Austin car erected near the cemetery entrance, had heard, correctly, that all grave-stones were to be removed to create a park but his statement that the Council's claim that the cemetery was full was untrue brought an immediate refutation from Roy Howell, the Town Clerk. He said that 'the cemetery was only full in the sense that there are no more new grave spaces to be sold and, therefore, somebody who has no previous connection with the cemetery will not be able to arrange their burial there'. He went on to say that there were a large number of graves in York Cemetery which were not full and members of families with burial rights could still be buried in them.[14] This was at variance with the result of the survey that Scott had made shortly before he ceased to be liquidator. A story that the whole cemetery was to be used to make room for a motor-way was more far-fetched as also was the information given to a visitor to the cemetery that all the occupants of war graves were to be exhumed and cremated.[15] With the lack of authoritative information from either the Corporation or the liquidator speculation of this sort was inevitable.

By April 1974 a draft agreement had been drawn up jointly by the Corporation and the liquidator and, although ratified by a Corporation committee, no firm date was fixed for its implementation, possibly because the Corporation had other more pressing matters to worry about, the ending of York's County Borough status and the setting up of the new District Council. When the Policy and Resources committee of the new organisation considered the cemetery agreement in August 1975 it decided that, at a time when it was trying to save money, it could not embark upon a project that would require it to take on extra staff and involve an estimated expenditure of £50,000, a decision greeted with regret by some York councillors and anger by some of its citizens who had relatives buried in the cemetery.[16] The liquidator now had no alternative but to proceed as had been originally intended as long ago as 1966, to dispose of as many assets as could be profitably realised for the benefit of the shareholders and then to abandon the cemetery. The dangerous state of the chapel was a continual worry but by October he had hit upon a solution which would solve this problem at no cost, even producing some profit. Very soon after the *volte-face* by the District Council he had negotiated a deal with a firm of masonry contractors who would buy the stone-yard and cottages for £2,000 and, for £1 a ton, remove all the monumental masonry and the stonework of the chapel, a grade II* listed building, together estimated to comprise some 5,000 tons.

Had she known of this development, Barbara Hutton, Secretary of the Georgian Society's historic buildings sub-committee, might well have been more outspoken in her report at the society's annual general meeting in 1975 instead of merely calling for some attention to be given to the structure to make it safe and water-tight before it got into a worse state.[17] Before Rushton could take this drastic step and let his contractor proceed he had to seek permission from the Companies Court where, early in 1976, the matter was once again stood over. Before the court hearing he had been informed by the Chancellor of the Diocese of York that the demolition of a chapel and the removal of grave-stones on consecrated ground could not be allowed without a faculty from the Consistory Court and he now had to decide if it was worthwhile seeking this or merely removing the grave-stones from the unconsecrated areas alone. Only 5¼ acres out of a total of 24 had not been consecrated but the contractor was still willing to remove all the stone, marble and granite from these areas.

By now the expenditure necessary to keep the cemetery operating was exceeding the income by a considerable amount and this deficit would have to be deducted from the balance of funds held to the credit of the cemetery company by the Bank of England, a situation that could not be contained for much longer from the rapidly dwindling funds. If Rushton was to apply for a faculty he would probably encounter considerable opposition from the relatives of those commemorated by the memorials and be involved in time consuming and expensive procedures which would further erode the credit balance. Further factors to be considered were the need, under the Town and Country Planning Act 1971, to seek permission to demolish a listed building and the costs of the Commonwealth War Graves Commission who had estimated that £10,812 would be needed to replace its headstones with a screen wall round the Cross of Sacrifice. All in all the difficulties were insuperable; the only practicable way forward would be to seek a simple disclaimer of the cemetery and its obligations whereupon the company would be finally wound up and its land vested in the Crown.[18] Ten years had now elapsed since the liquidation proceedings had started; the end was at last in sight but the final exequies would take another three years.

All maintenance work in the cemetery had ceased except in the area immediately round the entrance gate. Elsewhere the weeds were growing head-high, obscuring many graves and preventing relatives finding them. Worse still vandals were entering the cemetery and systematically pushing over headstones, opening coffins in the catacombs under the chapel and breaking into the other buildings. A small amount of vandalism had been a regular occurrence, with just a few stones damaged and some windows broken but new levels were experienced in February 1977 when over 50 graves were attacked. In May about 50 members of the Georgian Society made a visit to the cemetery and saw for themselves the depredations that were being made by time, the elements, the vandals and the thieves who had stolen every piece of lead from the chapel roof. They thought that a restored chapel could have a new life as a columbarium, a permanent repository for cremated remains, a facility that the City lacked. Perhaps, it was suggested, goats rather than fire could be used to control the vegetation. A year later, however, the Society changed its mind – goats were not the answer, they would strangle themselves with their tethers tangled round the monuments. The cemetery should be seen as 'a peaceful haven, mellowing with trees and bushes and wild flowers, and wild birds, conserving also its architecture, monuments, and aura of York's not-so distant history'. With this in mind the York Conservation Corps, formed in 1972, spent some time in the cemetery in February 1978 clearing away a fallen tree and transplanting sycamore and ash saplings, in a vain attempt to make it into an urban nature reserve. Later that year the most serious attack so far was made on the bodies in the catacombs. In July four coffins were pulled from their compartments under the chapel and rifled, it is thought, for jewellery. Undertakers had to be called in to re-inter the remains.[19]

The liquidator, while working towards the time when he could go to court for the final disclaimer proceedings, made every attempt to maximise the credit balance at the Bank of England. The stone-yard, outside the main boundary of the cemetery, was sold as a builder's yard. The monumental masonry showroom together with the forecourt immediately behind and to the north of the entrance gates became the property of Fred Emerson, a former cemetery employee, who set up his own monumental masonry business there, for £800. Two plots of land, in which no burials had been made, were sold to adjacent property owners and, perhaps most surprisingly, nearly all of the chapel woodwork, the pews, the dado panelling, the pilasters but not the floor-boards, was sold to a builder.

Finally, on 17 November 1978, Rushton presented his case to disclaim the cemetery. It was opposed by the Commonwealth War Graves Commission, the Crown Estates Commissioner and the holders of grave certificates. Neither York District Council nor the shareholders were represented in court. Despite the opposition Mr Justice Brightman gave leave for the liquidator to disclaim liability for the cemetery. A cemetery company operating for profit and paying large dividends, he said, had run it until its ground had become full, unprofitable and too expensive to maintain. At the end of the day one was left with a cemetery which should be treated with respect but there was nobody who wished to do the work. A disclaimer with no arrangements for the future would be most unsatisfactory but he had no jurisdiction to compel anyone to keep the cemetery in repair. However, in order to concentrate people's minds on what was going to happen when the disclaimer took place and allow time for arrangements to be made for some authority to take over the cemetery he delayed its application for several months. After the hearing a lawyer for the Crown Estates Commissioners explained that the Crown would become the formal owners of the bare estate but would not be responsible for any liabilities, neither would it take any action whatsoever to maintain the land.[20] It had taken nearly 12 years to reach this stage, seemingly a long time, but, in fact, par for the course. The proceedings for the City of Nottingham to take over the General Cemetery there had lasted ten years and those for Hull General Cemetery over thirteen.

In the event the delay to apply the disclaimer was fairly short. At the beginning of February 1979 Rushton announced that the cemetery would be locked on 16 February and a set of keys handed over to the Crown Estate Commissioners. On hearing this a storm broke out among people who had relatives buried in York cemetery. Tony Lister, a retired civil servant who had 13 brothers and sisters buried there, threatened, if the gates were locked, to break them down. He proposed to form a group to keep it open. Only Henry Thomas Atkinson, however, had the right, given to him by the judge, to apply in chambers for access to the cemetery.

He had represented the holders of grave certificates at the hearing. Nevertheless Lister, supported by other bereaved relatives, quickly held a series of meetings to attract others who wanted to join the fight against the closure of the cemetery. The protest group initially wanted to go further – to press for a public inquiry into the running of the cemetery before it went into liquidation and reveal who was responsible for 'the criminal neglect of this sacred burial ground'.

The immediate result was a temporary reprieve; the implementation date of the closure was delayed for a fortnight. The objectors, now formally constituted as the Bereaved Relatives Committee, decided to press the Council to take over the cemetery and make it a commercial proposition once again but its plea, at first, fell on deaf ears as the Council was not proposing to do anything which might imply that it was managing the cemetery. At the last minute, after the Policy and Resources Committee had met the Bereaved Relatives Committee, it was agreed that the Council would take charge of the cemetery keys and records as a short term solution only. This would ensure continued access and might even enable undertakers to make further burials. On 1 March the keys were handed over to Isaac Mullen, secretary of the Bereaved Relatives Committee, who had arranged for his brother, who lived in Cemetery Road, to open the gates every day. The first objective of the bereaved relatives had been achieved. Now they could turn their minds to the greater problem of clearing the site of uncontrolled vegetation and then keeping it tidy.[21]

Mr Rushton, the liquidator of York Cemetery Company, bowed out with a final act on the 12 April 1979, the signing of a formal order disclaiming all interest in 24 acres of freehold land, all implied covenants with holders of certificates conferring rights of burial in the cemetery, all contracts for the upkeep of graves and any obligations imposed upon the company by its agreements with the Commonwealth War Graves Commission. This act can have pleased nobody. The Crown Estate Commissioners now had a cemetery it did not want. The Commonwealth War Graves Commission had lost control of the war graves and the Cross of Sacrifice. York District Council had a liability within its boundary which it suspected might one day become a financial burden on its ratepayers. The bereaved relatives had no security for the future access. After 13 years of waiting the shareholders of the now wound up company, its assets all swallowed up by litigation, had failed to get any recompense. The future was indeed bleak.

York Council had said that to put the cemetery in order would cost £100,000, one of the principal reasons why it did not want to take it over. On the other hand it was willing to give some small financial support to the Bereaved Relatives Committee in its efforts to clear and tidy the site. Isaac Mullen, the Secretary of the committee, said 'It is a big job but it always looks larger to someone who doesn't want to do it. We are dedicated and determined to see it through, and will start work on Sunday, April 1, and work from then, every weekend, and evenings when we can, and we hope to have the job finished by the end of the summer'. The Committee were hoping that the Council would then change its mind and so, encouraged by other help offered, started with great enthusiasm, and great strides were quickly made in tackling the Herculean task. The bereaved relatives, a dedicated few, were joined by soldiers from Strensall and members of the York Sea Cadets and Air Training Corps. An offer of help was received from the Community Services Ancillary Officer who hoped to able to send four men serving community service orders made by the courts and the Manpower Services Commission agreed to provide some financial help under its Youth Opportunities Scheme so that ten out-of-work youngsters could be found employment for a year provided the Council reciprocated with cash, tools, and guidance. Last but not least, 15 members of York Youth Action, sponsored by the hour by their friends and relatives, came to the cemetery in July, for a day's gardening, armed with scythes and sickles.[22]

But this wholesale onslaught on the cemetery did not please everybody. The Yorkshire Naturalists' Trust, concerned at the loss of natural habitat, asked to meet the Bereaved Relatives Committee to try and reach an agreement about saving some of the older part of the cemetery and leaving it more or less as it was. In support of their case the Trust sent a copy of a report made by Dr Richard L. Gulliver, a natural history expert, which he had made shortly before the liquidation proceedings were completed. He thought that the consequence of a lack of maintenance for the previous 12 years, while causing some inconvenience to conventional visitors, had created a superb area for wildlife making York cemetery one of the finest urban nature reserves in existence. 'A visit to the cemetery', he said, 'is a relaxing and refreshing experience. It is an ideal tonic for the visitor wearied by the tourist round; or even for the resident exhausted by continuous shopping. It will appeal to anyone with even the slightest interest in wildlife and the countryside.' While birds, mammals, insects and wild flowers were all mentioned in Gulliver's report he had been mainly impressed by the variety of trees. He had found 25 varieties of trees represented by 160 specimens, nevertheless an 80% loss since the Ordnance Survey of 1889 when 827 trees were recorded. It was still an important collection and included London plane, false acacia and tulip trees, all rather uncommon in the north.[23]

While the naturalist's attitude to the clearing up was understandable the activity attracted a more unwelcome type of visitor, the vandal. Soon after work had started a number of headstones and crosses had been pushed over, not it was thought, by children, the monuments were far too heavy for them. Then in December 1979 more than 30 monuments including a 7ft high angel were smashed in another attack by people, in the words of the Bereaved Relatives' secretary 'sick in their minds'.[24] These memorials were not only a target for the vandals but parts of them, especially kerbs, made the maintenance work more difficult. The Bereaved Relatives sought permission from the Crown Estate Commissioners to remove them but were met with only sympathy and the Commission's admiration of their public spirit. The Commissioners had been advised that although they were now vested with the bare legal estate of the cemetery, if they refrained from exercising any act of ownership they could not be held liable for any of the burdens attached to the property. The giving of formal consent to remove kerbstones would constitute such an act of ownership.[25]

The Victorian Society was concerned about the deteriorating condition of the chapel which was, according to Sir Nikolaus Pevsner, a very fine example of the Victorian Greek revival style and it opened a file on it but did very little else. However, in June, as part of a membership recruitment drive, it called upon local architectural enthusiasts to lobby for its restoration.[26] The only body who could have responded to this lobby, York District Council, was much more concerned that its citizens should not be left with the responsibility for maintaining the resting place of the dead. Councillor Phillip Booth, at a meeting of the Policy and Resources Committee in July 1980, suggested that the time had come for dividing the cemetery into parts where there were living people who remember the dead and others where the graves meant nothing to anybody. Councillor Rodney Hills agreed that far too great a strain was imposed on the bereaved relatives but it would take a large sum to do anything about it. The committee at the end of its discussions, however, agreed that more suitable grass cutting machinery should be supplied for the Manpower Services Commission teams, who were, by now, bearing the brunt of the maintenance effort with occasional help from Community Service.[27]

The Manpower Services Commission scheme came to an end in June 1981 but one of its supervisors, John Snape, not wanting to see the work of his teams go to waste, started a scheme for the maintenance of individual graves. By June 1984 he had 600 customers on his register and was getting a grant from York Council which helped him to buy, among other things, herbicide to attack the weeds and undergrowth. The next month the M.P. for York, Conal Gregory, made his first visit to the cemetery and was shown round by its unofficial custodian. He, like John Snape, was concerned about the dangerous state of the chapel which was in an advanced state of decay. He wanted to see if it was worth restoring but thought the cost would be prohibitive. The cemetery, he said, 'was not a part of society that we should forget. It is a sad commentary on our times that it is in this state but, hopefully it can be made into a fitting memorial of the way various eras dealt with death.' Shortly after his visit the chapel was inspected by York Council's Chief Building Inspector, Henry Galpin, who agreed that it was indeed dangerous and recommended that it should be fenced off to protect members of the public visiting the cemetery. A few days later, at the end of July, in a very striking way, the chapel demonstrated just how dangerous it was. The roof collapsed bringing down part of the back wall.[28]

Snape had been attempting for some years to buy the cemetery from the Crown Estate Commissioners but their policy of not making any act of ownership meant that he had no prospect of success. Now, with the chapel in a demonstrably dangerous state, he thought there was no alternative but to demolish it, grass over the site and leave the burials in the catacombs undisturbed. Permission was needed for this, and, with the Crown Estate Commissioners sitting on the fence, he made an application to York Council who agreed to consider it despite hearing from the Commissioners that it was invalid as they had not given permission, surely an act of ownership.[29] This apparent slip was overlooked, perhaps because somebody wanting to protect the cemetery had appeared on the scene.

A number of residents of Belle Vue Terrace, living close to the cemetery, had been concerned for some time about its apparent neglect. The collapse of the chapel roof in August must then have been the catalyst that stirred them into action for, by October, with some other interested people, they had approached the Bereaved Relatives Committee and formed a new body, The Friends of York Cemetery. Its aims were threefold; to maintain it as a functioning cemetery with the preservation of burial rights granted by the liquidated company, to develop it as a centre for the discovery and interpretation of the 19th and 20th century history of York and to manage the habitat for nature study. The chapel was seen to have a vital role in this. After its restoration it would form a centre for the display of interpretive material and for genealogical studies as well as being a visual focus for the cemetery, playing a major role in education and tourism. In

After liquidation was completed in 1979 and the chapel was abandoned to its fate the vandals moved in. The chapel was obviously a target for their depredations. When this picture was taken in 1982 daylight could be seen through the damaged windows and the door.

[Photograph - Helen Kirk]

this latter role it could be seen as a natural extension of the York Story, part of York Castle Museum, housed in the church of St Mary, Castlegate. The grounds were a naturalistic landscape that both local residents and visitors could enjoy. A long term plan to achieve these objectives would need to be sustained by grant aid, fund-raising and voluntary labour, a programme that would demand much hard work by a dedicated few. [30]

There was no mention of any part for John Snape in these plans. For four years he had, almost single-handedly, been responsible for maintaining the cemetery and keeping all its paths open. In that time he had built up a grave maintenance business with 600 customers and, with the encouragement of all York's funeral directors, had co-operated with nearly 50 burials a year. He felt, quite strongly, that the Yorkshire Evening Press report on the formation of the Friends of York Cemetery was biased and had denigrated his own role which, to an extent, was at variance with that of the new group. He would have liked to see the buildings, which complemented the landscape so well, restored but, not having the funds for this, had applied for the chapel to be demolished. His clients, he thought, would not like their relatives' graves to be part of a nature reserve, encroached on

At the end of July 1984, shortly after the chapel was classified as a dangerous building, the roof collapsed. The public were warned to keep out by prominent notices placed in front of the portico.

The lead sheeting was stolen from the chapel roof, hastening the rot in the timbers which had started earlier. As a result of this the roof collapsed and the back wall, deprived of its support, was also damaged.

[Photograph - Dr. Richard Keesing]

by the wilderness, rather Pritchett's landscaping should be returned to its former clean cut lines by a committed professional. Not only was nature the enemy of Pritchett's vision; the vandals were keeping up their onslaught, having on one weekend in November, smashed between 30 and 40 headstones.[31]

The devastated interior of the chapel after the collapse of the roof. The bare brick work, has been revealed by the earlier removal of the timber dado and pilasters, sold during the liquidation period. The altar, at the east end of the consecrated area, was a later addition to the furnishings of the chapel.

[Photograph - Dr. Richard Keesing]

By July 1985 the Friends had decided grave maintenance and grave digging, the work so far carried out by Snape, would have to continue under any management plan and should contribute to the cemetery funds. At the same time more flesh was put on their original ideas. Ronald Sims, a York architect and a leading expert on the conservation of historic buildings, having visited the cemetery in March, had estimated that £141,000 would he needed to reroof the chapel and restore its interior and exterior to its 1837 appearance. The major portion of this cost would be met by English Heritage but financial help had been offered by other bodies, including York Civic Trust. The boundary walls of the cemetery approximately one mile in length, needed repair or replacement but York Community Project was willing to do this work for the cost of the materials only. While the land was to be run as a functioning cemetery it was to be managed on conservation lines following a carefully thought out, ecologically-balanced plan to be formulated by Askham Bryan College of Agriculture and Horticulture after consultation with the Yorkshire Wildlife Trust and other groups interested in conservation and ecology. The domestic part of the lodge was to be modernised and let as student accommodation while the office could house a full-time warden whose salary would be the major cost in the Friends plans but the provision of this post was essential to undertake and supervise the management plan, educational activities and burials.

The Friends of York Cemetery, the steering group set up in October 1984 to produce a long-term solution to the problems of the cemetery, wished to launch a larger, more broadly based society but, first, they revealed themselves as:

T. Beechey, Architect
K. Clark, Stonemason
F. Emerson, Monumental Mason
W. Fawcett, University Lecturer
R. Jenkinson, Solicitor
R. Keesing, University Lecturer
I. Mullen, Chairman, Bereaved Relatives
M. Rumsby, University Lecturer
F Stasiak, Teacher

They saw their role as a partnership between themselves and York Council. The Council would recover the freehold of the cemetery from the Crown Estate Commissioners and lease it to the Friends who would be responsible for implementing the management plan with a management committee of members from all the all interested bodies.[32]

Encouraged by the response to their proposals the Friends had constituted themselves into a Trust by June 1986 (the formal declaration was signed on 1 October 1986) and were seeking charitable status from the Charity Commissioners (granted 17 January 1989 as charity number 701091). Sufficient funds had now been accumulated to start some restoration work on the chapel; the rebuilding of the roof, necessary to stabilise the building and prevent further deterioration. The Askham Bryan management plan differentiated between the older and newer parts of the cemetery to allow contrasts to be developed in the natural history of the different parts, making for a more interesting and varied landscape, but it also demonstrated the need for control with carefully selected herbicides in carefully chosen areas rather than their random use. John Snape, who had agreed to give up his interest in seeking the freehold of the cemetery provided his livelihood was not affected, had used herbicides to destroy much of the shrub and flower life in the wilder parts of the land. The Friends now envisaged that he should continue his grave maintenance and grave-digging work provided he undertook not to spray or clear areas of the cemetery without the authority of the warden. The Friends' plan, which commanded broad sympathy from most political elements on York Council, was translated into practical effect by a grant of £5,000 towards the restoration of the chapel but included a sting in the tail with £1,100 for Snape to buy herbicides.[33]

The Policy and Resources Committee of the Council must nevertheless have had misgivings about becoming owners of the freehold of the cemetery, perhaps worried about what would happen if the Friends of York Cemetery Trust, at some time in the future, became defunct. This would then bring about the situation it had been trying to avoid for many years, full financial responsibility for an abandoned cemetery. Sensitive to this view the Friends applied to the Crown Estates Commissioner for the freehold to be transferred to them and proposed to the Charity Commissioners that a charitable company be formed, limited by guarantee, for the long term ownership and management of the cemetery. Membership of the company would be open to anyone interested in joining for a small annual subscription. The Council's involvement was revised to the provision of £16,500 a year for the salary of a warden and a part-time assistant together with a grant towards the purchase of maintenance machinery. As before there was to be a continued role for John Snape, working under a licence from the Friends.[34]

While these proposals brought the support in principle of the Policy and Resources Committee they did not appease John Snape. 'Who do the Friends of York Cemetery represent?' he asked, 'Do the bereaved relatives count for nothing?' Many of the members of his grave maintenance scheme wanted the cemetery to be just a cemetery and nothing else. He had applied to the Church of England for a licence to manage the consecrated part of the cemetery on behalf of the parishes under whose protection the ground lay, St Lawrence, York and St Oswald, Fulford, and was negotiating with the Crown Estates Commissioner for a similar privilege for the unconsecrated portions. In addition the Commonwealth War Graves Commission had recently appointed him to maintain the graves of the war dead buried in the cemetery. He had built up his business with a long hard struggle and he appealed to the citizens of York to come forward to help him in his fight to retain it. The Friends' proposal that, in return for a licence to continue his business, he should pay them 5% of his takings, particularly incensed him and he was not happy that the licence could be terminated for 'grossly inappropriate behaviour'. He was supported by Norman Stabler, a regular visitor to family graves in the cemetery who had had long discussions with Snape. Stabler thought that the cemetery should not become an area just for naturalists and that the restoration of the chapel was unnecessary in view of its derelict and dangerous state.[35]

The first concern of the Friends of York Cemetery, after they had purchased the cemetery, was to restore the chapel, a grade II* listed building. The new roof timbers were installed in 1987, the first stage of this task.

[Photograph - Dr. Richard Keesing]

The Policy and Resources Committee thought that the preservation of the chapel was essential, something that Snape could not do with his one-man operation. It preferred the Friends to run the site and wrote to Snape urging him to join forces with them. In October 1986 the Council agreed to back the Friends' proposals, provided they included a role for Snape which was agreeable to him, and made a grant of £11,000 a year for the next three years towards the salary of the warden and equipment. With Council support thus obtained the final stage to revive the cemetery was made on 13 February 1987 when the Crown Estate Commissioners conveyed the freehold of the cemetery to the Friends of York Cemetery, 24 acres, 'in consideration of the sum of £1' without any encumbrances.[36]

1987 opened with the appointment on 1 January of Paul levens as the first warden of York Cemetery, responsible for implementing and developing the ecological land management plan, supervising the York Council for Voluntary Service teams working on many projects within the cemetery, organising voluntary working parties and visits from schools and, finally, managing the funeral business. With grants and donations from English Heritage, The Pilgrim Trust, York City Council, The Joseph Rowntree Memorial Trust, The York Civic Trust, the Noel G. Terry Trust and H.B. Raylor Ltd the restoration of the chapel, a building rated by English Heritage as being among the top 8% of all the listed buildings in Britain, started with the erection of scaffolding on 9 July. Work started in earnest in August and the timberwork for the entire roof was completely installed by 22 September. After the roof was felted and battened it was slated by the end of November when the new ridge stones were cemented into place. Finally by mid January 1988 all lead work was complete and the first stage of the restoration was over. Real progress had been made and the Friends of York Cemetery could at last see some tangible evidence of nearly three years of discussions, negotiations and fund-raising when all they had to sustain them was a faith in the ultimate success of their efforts. The cemetery, neglected for so long, had been revived and its future was secure. An opportunity to celebrate the start of this most daunting task had arisen earlier, on 15 September, the 150th anniversary of the consecration of the chapel, when the Friends of York Cemetery held a lunch-time party to thank all the craftsmen, Y.C.V.S. workers and other people actively engaged in work on projects in the cemetery. Some 50 people came and enjoyed a light lunch of beer, bread and cheese. Much remained to be done but the first important step had been taken. From now on, with the experience gained, it would all be so much easier![37]

NOTES

1.   *Yorkshire Evening Press* 31 January 1967.
2.   YCA Acc 247, Notes of I. A. Scott Interview with R. W Boulton, n.d.
3.   YCA Acc. 247, Letter from R.W. Boulton to I.A. Scott, 26 September 1966.

4. *Yorkshire Evening Press* 31 January 1967.
5. *Yorkshire Evening Press* 6 July, 13 July 1967.
6. *Yorkshire Post* 8 September 1967.
7. YCA Acc. 247, Letter from I.A. Scott to York Undertakers, before 1 March 1969.
8. *Yorkshire Evening Press* 2 April 1968.
9. YCA Acc. 247, Letter from I.A. Scott to Board of Trade, 12 May 1969.
10. *Yorkshire Evening Press* 17 February 1970.
11. YCA Acc. 247, Letter from City Engineer to I. A. Scott, 12 February 1970, Letter from I.A. Scott to various undertakers, 13 February 1970, Letter from National Association of Funeral Directors to I.A. Scott, 17 March 1970.
12. *Yorkshire Evening Press* 10 January 1975.
13. YCA Acc. 247, Letter from I.A. Scott to Town Clerk, 20 August 1971, Letter from I. A. Scott to Board of Trade, 24 August 1971.
14. *Daily Telegraph* 30 November 1973; Yorkshire Evening Press 27 December 1973.
15. YCA Acc. 247, Letters from B. Allott, 31 January 1974, and FM. Broadhurst 21 July 1975.
16. *Yorkshire Evening Press* 2 September, 5 September 1975.
17. *Yorkshire Evening Press* 31 October 1975.
18. *Yorkshire Evening Press* 3 December 1975.
19. *Yorkshire Evening Press* 21 February, 10 May, 6 October 1977, 6 February, 2 May, 11 July 1978; York Georgian Society *Annual Report for 1977* p 7; *Annual Report for 1978* p 3.
20. *Yorkshire Evening Press* 18, 21 November 1978.
21. *Yorkshire Evening Press* 9, 10, 13, 16, 20, 24, 28 February, 2 March 1979.
22. *York Advertiser* 21 March 1979, 9 May 1979; Y*orkshire Evening Press Emergency Bulletin 30* April 1979; *Yorkshire Evening Press* 11 July, 16 July 1979; *Yorkshire Post* 12 July 1979.
23. Letter from Yorkshire Naturalists' Trust to Bereaved Relatives Committee, 3 May 1979.
24. *York District Advertiser* 9 May 1979; *Yorkshire Evening Press* 19 December 1979.
25. Letter from Crown Estate Commissioners to Bereaved Relatives Committee, 6 August 1979.
26. *Yorkshire Evening Press* 9 June 1979.
27. *Yorkshire Evening Press* 22 July 1980.
28. *Yorkshire Evening Press* 12 June 1981, 25 June, 23, 31 July 1984.
29. *Yorkshire Evening Press* Press 11 October 1984.
30. *Yorkshire Evening Press* 20 November 1984; *A Future for York's Victorian Cemetery* A discussion paper prepared by the Friends of York Cemetery in conjunction with the Bereaved Relatives Association, November 1984.
31. *Yorkshire Evening Press* 19 November, 3 December 1984.
32. Friends of York Cemetery *The Long-term Funding and Running of York Cemetery*, July 1985.
33. Friends of York Cemetery Trust, *Discussion Paper* 3 June 1986; *Yorkshire Evening Press* 24 June 1986; *Annual Report* Friends of York Cemetery Trust, 1987.
34. Friends of York Cemetery Trust, *Detailed Proposals for the Running and Management of York Cemetery*, Discussion Paper 4, 4 July 1986.
35. *Yorkshire Evening Press* 4, 7, 11 August 1986.
36. *Yorkshire Evening Press* 16 October 1986.
37. Annual Report 1987 York Cemetery Trust; *Yorkshire Evening Press* 7 September 1987.

7: 'Strong for Service Still' – The Future

His head,
Not yet by time completely silver'd o'er,
Bespoke him past the bounds of freakish youth,
But strong for service still, and unimpair'd

William Cowper The Task, book ii, The Timepiece

'From now on, with all the experience gained, it would be all so much easier' – brave words, closing the previous chapter, written in 1990 when the Trustees' plans for the future were fairly simple. In the short term these were the completion of the restoration of the chapel which in the fullness of time would play a major role in education and tourism, as a centre for the discovery and interpretation of the 19th and 20th century history of York through the medium of people buried there. It was intended that the site was to be developed as a habitat for the study of nature but burials could still take place, managed by the local undertakers under the benevolent eyes of the trustees, for those with rights, originally granted by the liquidated company but now restored. The long term plan for the achievement of these objectives could only be sustained by the efforts of the trustees in seeking grant aid and other funds to ensure the continued employment of the warden. He had been managing the site using much voluntary labour and supervising school visits with these ends in view since 1 January 1987, his salary largely paid by a grant from The City of York Council of £11,000 a year. This was initially for three years but it was hoped that the Council, recognizing the importance of the cemetery to the city, would continue its munificence for the foreseeable future. But, change was in the offing and these plans had eventually to be modified to meet the new circumstances.

The cemetery in 1988, a year after the Trust had taken over ownership. The volunteers recruited by the new warden have made valiant efforts to control the vegetation.

[Photograph - Richard Keesing]

First the restoration of the chapel had to be completed. The first phase of its restoration, the rebuilding of the collapsed walls and roof had been completed by January 1988 but there was still much more to do, particularly the refurbishment of the interior and repairs to the portico (phase 2), the restoration of the structure of the portico and securing the catacombs (phase 3) and improvements to the catacombs (phase 4). It had taken only six months to make the structure safe and watertight but phase 2 was to take much longer, not because of any inherent difficulties, but because English Heritage, who were contributing 70% of the cost of the project, required the highest standards of workmanship to ensure the long term future of the building. Workmen capable of these standards were in short supply and had many other commitments. Gaps in the flow of work were inevitable.

Phase 2 consisted of several major tasks. A suspended coffered ceiling had to be installed to replace the one destroyed when the roof collapsed. The damaged plaster cornice and capitals of the pilasters had to be repaired. The wooden pilasters themselves, the dado and door architrave, which had been stripped out after they had been sold by the liquidator, had to be replaced. A new level wooden floor in place of an earlier one with four pew platforms, which, in any case, had been affected by three years exposure to the weather after the roof collapse, had to be laid. New electric lighting and a power supply had to be provided. English Heritage architects visited the cemetery on 23 June 1988 to approve the proposals for the work prior to a grant towards the cost being made and work starting.

In February 1989 scaffolding was erected which enabled the plasterers to start repairing the cornices followed by the suspension, from the rafters above, of the 21 coffers which formed the new ceiling.

The reroofed chapel at the beginning of Phase 2.
[Photograph - Richard Keesing]

The plaster of the original ceiling had been some five inches thick, its weight contributing to the roof collapse. The new coffers were constructed of thinner but stronger fibre reinforced plaster which considerably lessened the load on the roof trusses. By May the work on the ceiling was complete and attention could turn to the laying of a concrete sub-floor which would not only support the wooden floor but also strengthen the whole building. By July the floor area had been prepared to receive the concrete which was supplied by Shepherd Construction free of charge. Working from the concrete sub-floor the plasterers returned in December to reconstruct the pilasters and built the new dado. The old one had consisted of vertical tongue and groove boards but it was replaced by plaster incised with horizontal and vertical lines to give it the appearance of stone blocks.

New wood for the floor would have been expensive but, in the event, sufficient seasoned pitch pine at 10% of the cost was recovered from a gymnasium, built in the 1930s by the Carnegie Physical Education College, now part of the Leeds Metropolitan University, which was being demolished. This was brought to the chapel in February 1990 for a short period of acclimatization before floor laying began in March. At first it had been intended to make an entrance to the catacombs from within the chapel with a staircase below the trapdoor where the lowering catafalque had once stood but this was now thought to be unnecessary.

Some of the coffers in position. The ceiling was completed by plastering the gaps between them.

[Photograph - Richard Keesing]

The plan, in undertaking all this work, was to restore the chapel to its 1837 appearance when there had been only natural lighting in the building. To preserve this effect nine concealed tungsten halogen 500 watt lamps were installed on the window sills which, when illuminated, filled the building with very even indirect light. Shepherd Construction very generously provided £2,000 towards the cost of the electrical installation and also supplied, at cost, the cable to connect the chapel to the electricity mains at the gatehouse. The final task, the decoration of the chapel, was completed in June 1991 by W.D. Bonney Ltd. The frieze was stencilled with its original pattern, the pilasters and door architrave were marbled and the stonework effect of the incised lines on the dado was enhanced by the individual "stones" being painted in subtly varying shades. Gold leaf, paid for with a grant of £500 from the York Civic Trust, was applied to the capitals and bases of the pilasters. Such was the standard of the decoration that W.D. Bonney Ltd won two awards, one from the National Federation of Painting and Decorating Contractors and the other made by the local branch of the Royal Institute of British Architects, who in October 1990 had presented a certificate for craftsmanship in stonework jointly to York Cemetery Trust, Ronald Sims, the architect, and the builders who had worked on the chapel. These awards were a very tangible recognition that the restoration of the chapel had achieved the standards required by the trustees and English Heritage.

To make the chapel usable for funerals and other events some linked stackable seating was required. Happily, in July 1990, York Minster was replacing the Czechoslovakian beech chairs in the nave with more comfortable and space-saving folding chairs and, for £3,000, an anonymous donor purchased 150 for the Trust. Two local undertakers also made small donations; Rymers gave a pair of coffin trestles and the North Yorkshire Co-operative Society a collection plate.

The interior of the chapel after it had been decorated and the chairs had arrived from York Minster.

[Photograph - Richard Keesing]

The decoration of the chapel had been completed in the nick of time. The York Georgian Society had, in January 1991, made a booking to hold a concert there later that year on 27 July. All was ready with just days to spare and the concert, attended by some 80 people, in effect celebrated the culmination of the hard work, undertaken by so many people, to restore the chapel to its 'pure Grecian revival classical proportions' that merited Grade II* listing. The concert, given by a York Georgian Society member, was described in the Society's annual report as 'a magical sensation, that of pure sound'. This sensation was produced by David Watkins, Principal Harpist with the London Philharmonic Orchestra and Professor of the Harp at the Guildhall School of Music. In a two-hour concert he played music ranging from the 16th century through to a conclusion with one of his own compositions. During his playing white fumes were seen emerging from the powerful lights on the window sills, and, as a safety precaution, they were switched off, one by one, until only a few remained lit. David Watkins, when asked afterwards if this had disturbed him, said it had not. Rather he had thought it was an intended artistic effect! On later investigation it was found that the problem was not an incipient fire but had been caused by the incineration of the bodies of insects attracted on the summer evening by the bright (and very hot) lights. With such a splendid inaugural event the official opening of the chapel on 20 September by Conal Gregory, MP for York, was almost an anticlimax.

Phase 3 of the chapel restoration, repairs to the interior faces of the fluted pillars of the portico and the installation of security grills over the windows and door of the catacombs, was completed between April and November 1993, largely with the help of a grant of £5,000 from the Feoffees of St Michael, Spurriergate. Altogether the first three phases had cost £183,974, all raised by grants obtained through the hard work and persistence of the Trustees led by their chairman, Dr Richard Keesing. (Phase 4, the final part of the chapel restoration was not, in fact, completed until June 2007 after repaving and painting and restoring the commemorative slate slabs closing the burial vaults) From an organisation that started with nothing, great things had been achieved but this was not the end – the gatehouse needed restoration and some new buildings were necessary.

Paul Ievens, not unexpectedly, resigned as warden on 2 January 1990. As a young man he had had to consider his long-term career prospects. Three years with the nascent Cemetery Trust had given him valuable management and organisational experience to add to his CV and he judged the time was right to move on, to the post of a lecturer in Horticulture at Riseholme College in Lincoln. During his time at York an on-going maintenance programme had been developed. This achieved there was next a need to concentrate on the non-grassed paths which urgently needed repair. Some, in fact, could be used to secure extra burial spaces. While many trees had been planted, with some losses in the dry 1989 summer, many more were needed. There had been an improvement in the wildlife in the cemetery as a result of the many species of plants sown and a new feature had been created called Bolton Percy. Under the guidance of Roger Brook, a lecturer at Askham Bryan Horticultural College, who had devised a low maintenance planting scheme in Bolton Percy churchyard, a similar area was laid out in the cemetery. An education programme had been developed and there were now 10 schools visiting regularly to grow

The boundary wall in the southeast corner of the cemetery was rebuilt in 1987 by Darren White and Frank Shaw Willauski.

seeds etc., and other higher educational establishments were also involved on the site. A major project undertaken during his wardenship had been the repair of the boundary wall in the southeast corner of the cemetery. After the liquidation period, because of its unsafe condition, York Council workmen had flattened the wall. During 1987 it was rebuilt by Darren White and Frank Shaw Willauski using 3000 bricks donated by Shepherd Construction with the remainder obtained from a dismantled colliery near Castleford. The work included the construction of Felicity Gate to allow access for pointing on the outside of the wall and also to let trustee, Felicity Stasiak, continue her walks from her home, across the cemetery, to Walmgate Stray. Last but not least burials had increased from 44 (including 8 cremated remains) in Ieven's first year to 64 (including 12 cremated remains) in his last year. During the same period grave plots sales had increased from 1 to 22. The people of York were beginning to notice that York Cemetery was back in business.

The Trustees acted with commendable speed in replacing Paul Ievens. Richard Lancaster, who had been managing a 200 acre park for Essex County Council, took over the role on 5 February 1990 commuting daily from Leeds. He was well qualified for the job with a degree in Third World Development. On 19 February he presented his ideas for the development of the site; many new trees, hedgerows and plants were to be introduced; the use of herbicides, growth retardants and other chemicals were to be kept to a minimum, only being used as a reluctant last resort; activities and games were to be provided on site, together with open play areas which would introduce school children to nature and its conservation; a pond with a marsh at one end was to be constructed, either at Belle Vue or near the gatehouse, to introduce an interesting new habitat; finally butterflies were to be encouraged by special planting along a south facing wall. He continued the maintenance and education programmes started by his predecessor but unfortunately before he could develop any of his ideas, apart from deciding that the pond should be at least 5 x 5 metres in size and preparing a list of required trees, he resigned on 31 October to take up a post as a Senior Countryside Ranger with Leeds City Council managing a 700 acre site.

There were 14 applicants for the warden's post and from them Bill Shaw was selected. A graduate of Leeds University and a one-time countryside ranger, Shaw was, at the time of his application, running a smallholding near Bridlington but wanted to come to York so that his children could attend the Quaker schools in the City. He took up his new duties on 3 December 1990 and was ready to present his initial thoughts on the management of the site by 17 December. He proposed to continue the two schemes suggested by his predecessor, the butterfly walk planted with trees, shrubs, herbs and flowers attractive to that species, and the construction of a pond to be topped up with ecologically sound water channelled from the gatehouse roof. His major concern, again building on the work of the previous wardens, was to break up the virtually treeless, modern area of the cemetery with hedges and tree stands. English native species, particularly beech, birch, aspen oak and hazel, in contrast to the exotic species in the Victorian section, should be introduced. In future they would, perhaps, produce fuel for a wood-burning heating stove that he thought should be installed to provide some warmth in the gatehouse. A burial area specifically for cremated remains should be created in the semi-circular area between the Park gates in Cemetery Road backed with colourful bushes and flowering plants.

The herb garden in September 1994. Kerbs have been added to all graves but the beech hedge has not yet been planted

By May 1991 Shaw and the volunteers he had already recruited had planted 1448 trees and shrubs, including some Chusan palms from China and a number of eucalyptus species from Australia. This was just the beginning of a three year plan. The volunteers, who came in to work as a team on Saturday mornings, had also started work preparing a cruciform shaped herb garden in the south-east part of the cemetery and the butterfly walk along the northern boundary wall where it would enjoy considerable sunlight. The latter immediately attracted a grant of £240 from the York Vikings Rotary Club, followed in October by £200 from Forte plc's community chest, in November that year by £284 from English Nature and, later, in November 1992, by £260 from the Prince's Trust. The Lord Mayor of York, Councillor Ann Reid, formally opened it on 27 August 1993. While work on the herb garden started in March 1991 and the turfs that had overgrown the graves in the selected area were removed in the next month it was not until March 1994 that the individual herb beds were created by adding kerbs to the graves that had not previously had them, creating paths between them and surrounding the whole area with a beech hedge. It was given new impetus in July that year by the arrival of Ruth Sheratt, a herbalist, under whose guidance it became a Physic garden consisting largely of medicinal herbs. She intended that, with sponsorship that never, in fact, materialised, it should be of commercial benefit to the cemetery. Now, enhanced with plants with culinary uses and the individual beds marked with stones carved by Steve Basten, a trainee mason, it exists as an interesting feature.

A wildlife bathing and drinking station ready for use in May 1992

The warden's work programme for 1992 included the construction of the pond and the provision of wildlife drinking and bathing stations. By the end of the year a 13 x 8 metre butyl lined pond had been created with the help of a grant of £930 from British Gas Grassroots Action Scheme. In the following spring it was seeded with imported frog spawn. The tadpoles which hatched are the progenitors of a thriving population of frogs which return to the pond every year to lay their eggs. Landscaping, including paving, plants and a seat, to make it fit in with the lawned areas at the front of the cemetery, was completed later in 1993. Shell Better Britain had agreed in November 1991 to make a grant of £367 towards the installation of cast iron baths at six locations round the cemetery to provide drinking and washing water for wildlife in areas remote from the pond. The baths, rendered with a cement and dung mixture, were set into the ground and provided with a ramp of stones which would allow any animals falling in to escape. In January

1992 Nestlés made a grant of £100 towards the purchase of 12 rubbish barrels. They were painted and lettered by students from York College; black for waste and grey for compostable materials and they were placed in pairs in six locations round the site.

The start of the Scented Walk, marked by a stone carved by Fred Emerson

Projects to beautify or add interest to the site were generated thick and fast. Some, like a maze amongst the gravestones in the Victorian section, did not find approval from the trustees. All schemes were required to have been assessed to ensure that there was a proper budget for their implementation and the means within the organisation for their future maintenance. Some took a long time to come to fruition. A proposal from Dr James Merryweather, a biologist at York University, made in January 1993, to construct a fernery and stock it with a wide variety of species was approved but it was not opened until October 2002 when Geoffrey Smith, a TV gardening expert and creator of Harlow Carr Gardens at Harrogate, was invited to perform the task. A Scented Walk lined with plants that could be smelt and felt by visually handicapped persons did commend itself to the trustees. In July 1993 English Nature offered a grant of £5,000 for its construction which was to be undertaken with the help of disabled people. With its entrance marked by a stone carved by Fred Emerson, it was officially opened by the Lord Mayor, Councillor David Wilde, on 16 May 1995, although it had already been in use for nearly a year. The rockery made by Backhouse Nurseries in 1924 on the northern boundary of the Lawn Park Section had, over the intervening years, become overgrown with weeds and self-seeded trees. Its rebuilding, with some additional millstone grit boulders and replanting, started in January 1995 as part of the Woolwich Action Earth Challenge sponsored by the Woolwich Building Society. Further funding was provided by the City of York Council (£500) and Action Earth (£100). Two years later on 17 February 1997, to mark the 10th anniversary of York Cemetery Trust's ownership of the site it was re-opened by Professor Alistair Fitter from the Biology Department of the University of York.

Many volunteers helped with all this work, supplemented quite considerably by many other not-so-willing volunteers participating in employment schemes. Some came to the cemetery under Employment Action, a scheme aimed at getting people, who had been unemployed for over six months, back into work. The Yorkshire Rural Community sent people with physical or learning difficulties. A Government Training Scheme provided 16-18 year olds with employment experience. The Trident Trust found that the 1-3 week placements, for pupils at colleges and schools, which the cemetery could offer were a useful introduction to the world of work. Community Action, acting as agents for the Training and Enterprise Council, also found work in the cemetery for the long-term unemployed. The Community Service Unit of the North Yorkshire Probationary Service sent offenders from the Courts, either in gangs or individually as skilled workers, to repay their debts to society. Also in this category came the women from Askham Grange Open Prison who were easing their way back into the real world after having completed the bulk of their sentences. With all these sources of help at his beck and call Bill Shaw was to say, in May 1994, "We have plenty of labour but not enough machines".

From this source of manpower came, not only the workers, but the supervisors and project leaders who allowed the warden time to plan the work programme, to seek funding for the projects and exercise the control over all that was happening in the cemetery. From this pool he was able to find supervisors for both the able-bodied and handicapped workers; planners of events, concerts, art exhibitions and workshops to be held in the chapel and its immediate environs; project leaders for the schemes that enhanced the site; investigators who could determine how the disposition of graves in the cemetery corresponded with the intended plan and what unused burial space was available; fund raisers and educational assistants to relieve some of the burden thrust upon the paid, but part-time, education officer in organising and preparing projects for school visits.

The first warden had dealt with school visits himself but shortly after the arrival of the second warden it was realised that this aspect of his work was growing to such an extent that other work would suffer. Accordingly it was decided to appoint an education officer to relieve him of the direct supervision and organisation of school visits. Two grants, each of £2,000, had been obtained from the Rowntree Trust and the Ernest Cook Trust which would fund this appointment for some two years. The first education officer employed by York Cemetery Trust was Anne Mattam, a qualified geography teacher, who began her duties at the cemetery in April 1990, working seven hours a week usually on Tuesday and Thursday mornings. She left in August 1991 having prepared trails in the cemetery and a work package based on information from the cemetery registers which fitted well into the National Curriculum attainment targets. She was followed by a sequence of equally dedicated education officers who expanded on her initial plans. By July 1992 the money earmarked to pay the education officer was running low and new income was essential to maintain the burgeoning education service, possibly from the local education authority. A grant of £500 in April 1993 from the Colin & Sylvia Shepherd Trust came to the rescue of the service just in time and would ensure continuity of employment for the education officer for a further six months, now at ten hours a week. While the service was appreciated by the schools who visited the cemetery, the facilities on site, particularly the toilets, were not. Nevertheless by 1995 the education service was booming with visits from schools both local to, and from outside York. The vexed question, however, was still the problem of finding money to pay the education officer. Grants for equipment for the education room were more successful with Rowntree's providing £2,000 and York Common Good Trust £200.

By September 1996 the education service was at a crossroads, the victim of its own success. That there was money available to pay the wages of the education officer, now increased from 10 to 15 hours a week, was almost entirely due to the allocation of the interest earned from the cemetery's deposit account to the education fund. The Assistant Director of Education in York suggested that a Victorian Historical package could be prepared for junior schools as part of their curricula. This would involve regular visits to the cemetery of up to 240 children on four days a week during the summer term. A classroom on site was needed to provide facilities for teaching, working, eating and keeping dry. In return the City of York Council would provide funding to cover the cost of salaries and consumables. With this tempting offer dangling before it the Trust decided that the chapel catacombs could be transformed into a classroom with seminar areas in the unused arched vaults. They were, however, extremely damp due to water leaching through its walls which were below ground level. If they were to be used by children this problem would have to be solved. In July 1998 the Feoffees of St Michael, Spurriergate, provided a grant of £10,000 towards the tanking and external drainage of the catacombs which was completed by May 1999 at a total cost of £16,963, the balance being found from the Trust's own resources. Then in September an unsuccessful application was made to the Heritage Lottery Fund for funding to provide salaries for a full-time education officer and part-time staff. With the failure of this application, and, after employing a consultant in 2002 to advise on the educational potential of the cemetery, it was reluctantly decided to suspend the education service. Schools were becoming increasingly unwilling to leave the security of their own buildings to avoid the costs and difficulties of providing the extra supervision for outside visits. The consultants had suggested adult education was the way forward but this too had a cost implication that the Trust could not meet.

As early as 1988 a firm of antiquarian booksellers had asked the Trust if it could rent part of the gatehouse for its business. It was, of course, necessary to retain part of the gatehouse as an office for the warden, but letting out a considerable part of it had always formed part of the Trust's plans for earning income from the site to contribute towards the warden's salary, and to pay for the other expenses of running the site. There was, however, one snag that prevented an immediate lease being negotiated. The gatehouse was in need of major restoration work to the roof, structure and the basement which lay beneath the water table of the cemetery and was often flooded. It was estimated that the structural work would cost £31,395 with a further £10,000 needed to bring the interior up to a letting standard but the Trust did not have this sort of money available. A loan, hopefully interest free, would be required.

Other organisations showed interest in using the gatehouse. The Yorkshire Museum wanted to use it as a training centre. A computer firm wanted to establish its business there and, best of all, would raise the funds for its refurbishment. After a euphoric month the Trust's hopes were dashed when the firm withdrew its offer. A group of office designers were very keen to move in by 9 April 1993,

The pond nears completion in February 1993 while the site for the tool shed beyond it is being prepared.

a date that could not be realised due to the vexed question of finding money for the work. English Heritage, who had provided 70% of the cost of restoring the chapel, would not contribute to the 1837 gatehouse, despite the fact that it was a Grade II listed building, as it thought that the later additions to the north and south ends of the building had compromised its integrity. In June the City of York Council proposed that it would provide the funding so that the letting income would be uncompromised but this was, at the time, conditional on a tenant first being secured. Shortly afterwards Ronald Sims took over as architect for the restoration. Planning permission and listed building consent was given in January 1994, tenders for the work were sought in February and work started on the roof in September. The total cost of the work would not, it was thought, exceed £80,000, In the event, when the work was completed at the end of 1995 it had cost just over £100,000, but this included a new tool store between the gatehouse and the pond. The Council provided half of this amount, now on condition that it would cease making its annual grant of £10,580 from the Planning Committee's very small Greening budget towards the warden's salary. This had continued at the same level, without any regard for inflation, since the Trust took over the cemetery. York Cemetery Trust found the other half of the money from its reserves built up from the sale of grave plots. It took until September 1998 to find a tenant but, happily, the gatehouse has been occupied and provided valuable income continuously since then.

By October 1994 the walls and roof timbers of the tool shed were in place.

With the City of York withdrawing its support for the cemetery at the end of 1995 York Cemetery Trust was now thrust on its own resources and had to find all the income to run the site. A major change in the Trust's plans, however, had taken place in February 1994, a considerable alteration to its original intentions but nevertheless a change which ensured its financial survival. When it took over the cemetery in 1987 the Trust had had to grant a licence to John Snape who had, in the years following the completion of the liquidation of the old cemetery company, established a grave digging and maintenance business on the site. He was to prove to be a continuous source of aggravation for the Trust. He assumed that his licence gave him the sole rights to dig graves and in March 1989 had an altercation with an undertaker who brought in his own gravedigger as Snape was charging more to dig graves at York Cemetery than elsewhere. More complaints followed concerning the standard of his work so the locks on the cemetery gates were changed to ensure that he could only work on site while the warden was on duty. In April 1991 it was decided to revoke his licence but Snape was determined to go to arbitration to resolve the matter. Although an arbitrator was appointed in May 1992 the two parties to the dispute were not brought together. It was Snape himself who provided the eventual solution to the problem by proposing, on 19 August 1992, that he would relinquish all his interests in the cemetery, grave digging and grave maintenance for both private individuals and the Commonwealth War Graves Commission, for just £500 although he had previously valued his licence at £30,000! This was quickly agreed and from 17 February 1994 York Cemetery Trust began its burial business having taken over the grave maintenance business in May the previous year. These new activities were to provide it with sufficient new income, even after appointing its own gravedigger, Alan Morgan, on 31 January 1994, to more than replace the Council grant. In fact the additional income has also allowed, since September 1997, the employment of another member of staff to help with the increasing number of graves being maintained.

While the negotiations to purchase the burial and grave maintenance business from Snape were proceeding the two parties plus the Friends of York Cemetery were involved in a related matter, the legality of their various activities on the site. Snape had applied to the Registrar for the Province and Diocese of York on 20 January 1986 for a faculty to maintain and dig graves in the cemetery but it had not been progressed, awaiting an associated application from the Friends of York Cemetery. This was required to allow the Friends to manage the cemetery and license Snape to continue his business there after it had had the ownership transferred to it from the Crown Commissioner. Although this transfer happened in February 1987 Snape and representatives of the Trust did not appear in the Consistory Court in York Minster before the Chancellor of the Diocese until 19 February 1991 to enable all outstanding matters to be regularised. The outcome was that Snape's right to carry on his business was confirmed, the agreement of 19 August 1992 was approved and he was granted the right to continue his activities to 17 February 1994 when he would finally relinquished his licence. The Trust and Friends were granted a confirmatory and ongoing faculty covering its previous and future activities in the consecrated part of the site which allowed the two bodies :-

1   to restore, repair and maintain the consecrated part of the chapel. A new faculty would, however, be required if its internal or external appearance was to be altered.

2   to run the cemetery in accordance with its properly constituted Regulations which formed an attachment to the faculty.

3   to carry out routine maintenance on memorials and make alterations to paths, walls, trees and car parks that were not inconsistent with the consecrated nature of the land and would not cause offence or scandal to Christian people or bereaved relatives.

4   to use the chapel for burial services for all faiths or none, provided that it did not extend to other non-Christian services. Musical, dramatic and social functions and exhibitions were allowed provided they did not cause offence in a partly consecrated building.

5   to re-order the memorials in the cemetery in accordance with the Regulations.

6   to allow graves spaces to be reserved.

7   to promote educational activities which did not interfere with the cemetery's function as a burial ground.

8   to make charges in accordance with the Regulations. These charges could be altered if approved by the Trust and the Friends.

The Chancellor apportioned the costs of this hearing and the work undertaken in the Registrar's office on a 75/25% basis. Unhappily for Snape his 25% share was more than he had received from the Trust when it bought his business! On being asked what would happen if he did not pay the Chancellor replied "We will cross that bridge when we come to it".

Three toilets had been built in the gatehouse as part of the restoration and, while these relieved the problem for school visits, they were not readily accessible by the general public who came to the cemetery or the participants in the many events held on site. An application was made to the Foundation for Sports and the Arts who, in February 1996, awarded York Cemetery Trust a grant of £25,000 for the provision of public toilets to be built on to the north end of the tool store. The building work started in May 1997 and was completed by November at a total cost of £43,409, the extra funding provided by The York Challenge Fund (£12,500), The Colin and Sylvia Shepherd Trust (£1,000), The Guildhall South Neighbourhood Forum (£1,000) and The York Common Good Trust (£200). Ralph Kaner, chairman of the York Challenge Fund, officially opened it later in the year. The new building had included a space for a retail kiosk where it was hoped flowers and plants could be provided for people tending their family graves. Initially a lease for one year was let in November 1997 to a local florist in Fishergate who failed to put any effort into selling on the site. The lease was terminated by mutual agreement in February 1998 and until September 1999, with the limited resources available to him, the warden tried to provide this service. However, shortly afterwards, a new lease was agreed with two ladies trading as Acorns Flowers and they opened for business on 1 December. Nearly eight years on Acorns is still trading, not only offering a service to cemetery visitors, but also providing a presence and a contact point at the cemetery at weekends and at other times when the cemetery office is closed.

The tool store, flower kiosk and public toilet block in June 2003.

[Photograph - Hugh Murray]

The cemetery entered the electronic age with its own website in 1998. Jared Smith, an undergraduate at Horsforth College, Leeds, reading for a degree in media studies, needed to design and launch a website with some archival content on to the internet. He visited the cemetery in March 1998 to discuss what was required from both his and the cemetery's point of view and in September, after he was awarded his degree, he presented his work to the Trust. For over eight years his website was the international showcase for York Cemetery. It informed enquirers of all the activities on the site, the history of the cemetery and the facilities it offered. The archive aspect was covered by the inclusion of a virtual military trail which led the user round a number of monuments commemorating soldiers, sailors and airmen who had been connected with conflicts from the Crimean War the Second World War. Although a totally new website (www.yorkcemetery.org.uk) was introduced late in 2006 the basis of Jared Smith's design still lives on in the companion genealogical site (www.yorkcemeterygenealogy.co.uk).

In 1999 an anomaly, which had beset York Cemetery Trust for a long time, was resolved. The original intention in 1984 was that there would be one organisation, a charity, to be called the Friends of York Cemetery Trust who would own and manage the cemetery. When an application for charitable status was made to the Charity Commissioners (Liverpool) in 1986 the Friends were surprised to learn that a charity could not own consecrated land and this formed some two thirds of the cemetery. The solution was to split into two separate groups, York Cemetery Trust, who would own the site and employ the staff, and The Friends of York Cemetery who would become a charity and be responsible for seeking grants and raising funds. This solution was acceptable to the Charity Commissioners and there the matter rested for over a decade when it was learnt that Highgate Cemetery was owned by a charity. A new application was made to Liverpool only to receive the same answer but, on asking how Highgate had gained charitable status, the Liverpool office referred the matter to its head office in London. Whether or not the regulations had changed since the first application was not revealed but charities could now, indeed, own consecrated land. The ultimate result was that York Cemetery Trust became registered charity No 1075408 on 10 May 1999! While it would, perhaps, have been possible to go back to the original intention and have only one body responsible for all activities it was decided, as the Trust and the Friends were constituted differently and had, over the years, established their own satisfactory and non-conflicting ways of working, to preserve the *status quo*. While the Friends have provided, over the years, grave digging equipment and tools and machinery for use on the site some of their major contributions have been the renewal of the tarmac on the main drive to the chapel, the restoration of Belle Vue Gates and the relighting of the chapel with high intensity arc lights.

One of the major activities undertaken by the Friends was informing the world that York Cemetery still existed as a burial ground and had taken on a new role as a community amenity. This was done by regular Sunday guided walks from April to October each year for members of the public. These were started by Hugh Murray in 1988. At first the theme of the walks was historical, dealing with the creation of the cemetery, the demise of the private company and its

The Forest of Galtres Society being led on a guided walk in 1992 by Hugh Murray. This area was shortly afterwards planted out to become part of the Butterfly Walk.

future under the Trust. Later the programme, which still continues today, was extended to include a wide variety of subjects, amongst other things, geology, wildlife, photography and genealogy. A large number of private societies, from gardening clubs to women's institutes, from historical societies to conservation organisations, have also included a visit to the cemetery for a guided walk as part of their summer syllabuses. For a period between 1989 and 1991 guided tours were also offered on Tuesday evenings as well, ostensibly to offer an alternative evening entertainment for visitors to York staying in guest houses and hotels but also to try and ward off the possibility of one of York's providers of ghost walks muscling in on the territory. The prospect of actors, dressed as skeletons and leaping out from behind tombstones on to the unwary walkers, could not be contemplated. It was far from the dignified ethos which the Trust wished to cultivate. These walks were aimed mainly at adults. More formal education for children was offered by the education officer as recounted earlier in this chapter.

Bill Shaw resigned on 18 May 1999 to seek a new challenge after having managed the cemetery for over eight years, a period in which much had been achieved. The landscape of the cemetery had been enhanced, not only had the appearance of the modern section been changed by the planting of trees which were now beginning to make their presence felt but many plants and flowers had been introduced, including over 2,000 bulbs on 1 November 1997 as a memorial to Princess Diana. Many new features had been introduced, the scented walk, the butterfly walk, the herb garden, the remembrance garden for cremated remains and the pond, twice since rebuilt, while the rockery had been rescued from its abandoned state. He had had to control the volunteers and other people who were involved in all this work while working in the building site of gatehouse restoration and tool shed and toilet construction. And, in the middle of all this, his workload had been increased by the acquisition of the burial and grave maintenance business which required the employment of two new members of staff.

One project he initiated, specifically to celebrate the millennium in 2000, but could not see through to completion, was the reinstallation of the chapel bell to its home under the portico roof. It was lying, forlorn and forgotten, in the catacombs after it was taken down while the timbers of the portico were renewed. Its replacement would leave only the catacombs needing work finally to complete the restoration of the chapel. Shaw's successor was Hugh Goudge selected from 56 applicants. He was a retired Regimental Sergeant Major in the Rifle Brigade and a tree warden in London who had taken a degree in conservation on entering civilian life so that he could further his particular interest in trees. He started work at the cemetery on 2 June 1999.

An estimate of £2,000 for the restoration of the bell had been received from a local bell expert in May 1998 but this had been revised to £2,610 in September 1999. Goudge, however, proposed, that the work should be undertaken by cemetery volunteers under the auspices of the Friends of York Cemetery who readily agreed to his proposal. The project, relaunched early in 2000, seized the imagination of the Friends, volunteers, businesses and local people and, very quickly, cash donations of £1,843 had been received while Bootham Engineers donated the metal frame to support the bell in the portico. The reinstalled bell was rededicated on 16 September 2000 by the Right Reverend Humphrey Taylor, Bishop of Selby, in the presence of the Lord Mayor of York, Councillor Shân Braund. The Salvation Army's York Citadel Salvation Band provided the music at the ceremony.

Hugh Goudge left on 18 October 2002 to set up his own tree surgery business in Wakefield. Six people were short-listed for interview from the 30 applications received in response to advertisements in the local and national press. From these

Vanessa Temple, a graduate in Countryside Management from Bishop Burton Agricultural College who was working as a park ranger in Hull, was selected and she started work in the cemetery on 21 October. Like her predecessor her main task is to manage the site and maintain the features that had been introduced in the earlier years of the York Cemetery Trust's ownership and, most importantly, the burial and grave maintenance business. This business, together with rental from the gatehouse and the flower shop are the Trust's principal sources of income and are vital to pay the wages of the staff, now four, having been joined by an office administrator in July 2003. An investigation to find unused graves available for burial both from within the numbered spaces on the plans drawn by the Trust's predecessor, the York Public Cemetery Company, and by a more creative use of other areas on the site has confirmed that, for the foreseeable future, York Cemetery Trust can continue to offer burial facilities for those who wish to spend eternity in a place managed on ecological principles which provides a habitat for wildlife, a protected environment which also offers opportunities for conservation activities, education, and informal recreation.

Phoenix-like from the ashes of the liquidated cemetery company the new organisation has emerged, the initiative of a dedicated band of volunteers, whose efforts, together with those of the cemetery staff, should ensure many long years of existence. It is hoped that there will be no further catastrophes requiring regeneration.

Appendix 1

The Register Database

From 21 January 1837 to the present day a record of all the burials in York Cemetery has been maintained continuously in 20 registers, each containing an average of 6,500 entries. As an aid to finding entries in these registers the clerk in the office of the York Public Cemetery Company compiled rudimentary index books in which the surnames of the deceased were entered in date order of burial in the section for the initial letter of the surname. Thus in the Bs, Bainton could follow Bygrave and next could come Brown, Bishop etc. In all, 12 of these indexes were compiled but, even with their help, the search for a particular individual or a group of family members could be laborious and time consuming and there was always the possibility that a vital entry had been missed. When the York Cemetery Trust set up its office on site it was equipped with microfilms of the registers and indexes copied by the Church of Latter Day Saints from the originals held in the City of York Archives. Using a reader purchased by the Friends of York Cemetery these microfilms were used, at the expense of the wardens' other more important duties, to provide a service to genealogists and family members arriving at the cemetery to look for ancestors buried there.

If the records could be entered on a computer database a considerably more efficient and comprehensive service could be offered but the scale of the task of entering over 120,000 records on to a computer was daunting and no real effort was made to explore the problems that had to be overcome to achieve the desired result. Then, in April 1993, came the catalyst that was to set the data recording process in motion. Dr Andrew (Bone) Jones, at that time director of the Archaeological Resource Centre (ARC) in St Saviour's Church, was putting together an archive of information about the parish in which his centre was situated. He knew that the cemetery registers would contain information about the parishioners of St Saviour's who were buried in York Cemetery after the parish graveyard had closed and invited Hugh Murray to the ARC to discuss the possibility of computerising the cemetery registers to make this information accessible. The outcome of this discussion was a project to which York Cemetery Trust readily agreed. The ARC would provided the work space where the data would be input and the original registers could be securely stored, York Cemetery Trust would staff the project from Employment Action and Hugh Murray, who provided the computer, and David Poole would supervise the scheme.

The objectives of the project were to make the records of York Cemetery more accessible for genealogists and family historians by providing a single alphabetical index by surname, forenames, death date and age. It was further thought that the database could provide researchers, teachers and students with information on causes of death in York 1837-1927, infant mortality, epidemics in York, life expectancy, comparative mortality of the various strata of society as defined by their places of residence etc. The possibility of linking the database with photographs of the graves in the cemetery and their occupants was also foreseen in defining the project.

While data inputting nominally started in July 1993 it was not until the recruitment in May 1994 of Sue Degnan, the first of a series of Employment Action staff, that work started in earnest. She completed the first register by December and from then onwards work proceeded at a steady pace, with David Poole assisting with inputting, until completion of the twentieth and current register in 1998. By this time new ideas on the use of the database had developed. With the register recording completed, the two supervisors, now working without any other help, first linked the register with the index of Monumental Inscriptions (MIs) recorded by the York and District Family History Society, a task which it had started on 19 June 1979. At first the idea was merely to indicate if a person buried in the cemetery was commemorated on a monument but it was soon realised that it would be of much greater benefit if the result of a search in the database for an individual or a grave also displayed the full wording of the MI. The intention of the Family History Society was to complete its recording of the whole cemetery by the millennium year but it was well behind schedule for this. The task was, however, completed in November 1999 entirely due to the perseverance of David Poole who recorded the greater part of the modern section on his own. He has since rechecked the earlier recorded areas and, as a result, many hundreds of additional monuments have been added to the records. In September 2000 another data recording project was started, listing the grave purchase details for private graves, to be followed by the recording of the stillbirth registers.

David Poole, at the Archaeological Resource Centre, inputting data from the registers

In the course of ten years or more work on the cemetery database much experience was gained by the two supervisors. This has enabled Hugh Murray to modify the database search programmes he had written to take into account the anomalies and idiosyncrasies of the original registers. Additional databases of multiple grave plots, surnames and alternative spellings of them, and people commemorated but not buried in York Cemetery were compiled and linked with the main database. Much information wrongly entered in the original registers by the York Public Cemetery Company's office staff has been corrected. Finally, in fulfilment of one of the original objectives, a start was made in 2006 to collect photographs of the people buried in the cemetery. York Cemetery now has a database which is probably unique among all cemeteries, bringing together many sources of information to ensure that researchers and enquirers are given the fullest possible answer to their enquiries as well as providing a very valuable management tool for the cemetery.